Leadership
in Christian Ministry

James E. Means

BAKER BOOK HOUSE
Grand Rapids, Michigan 49516

Third printing, October 1993

Printed in the United States of America

Unless otherwise noted, Scripture references are from the Holy Bible: New International Version © copyright 1973, 1978, 1984 the International Bible Society. Used by permission of Zondervan Bible Publishers. Other translations cited are the King James Version (KJV), the Revised Standard Version (RSV), and Today's English Version (TEV).

Library of Congress Cataloging-in-Publication Data

Means, James E.
    Leadership in Christian ministry / James E. Means.
       p. cm.
    Includes index.
    ISBN 0-8010-6250-0
    1. Christian leadership. I. Title.
BV652.1.M44   1989
262'.1—dc20   89-7024
                                                           CIP

To **Barbara**

a special gift of God

Contents

Foreword

Twenty-five years ago books on leadership from a Christian point of view were all but nonexistent. Thanks to the effort of authors like Jim Means, that condition has been reversed. Not only has he adequately treated the organizational aspects of church management, but he has done so with acute sensitivity to the spiritual dimension. In short, this book properly deals with the church as both organization and organism.

Leadership in Christian Ministry is well organized, well balanced, and well written. Means puts his finger on problem areas: pastor–lay leader struggles, shepherding, and the practice of servant-leadership. He offers a welcomed condemnation of manipulative techniques and calls for mutual accountability on the part of all Christian leaders.

My favorite emphasis centers on team leadership and consensus decision making, a leadership function addressed in part 3. Replete with examples and support texts, *Leadership in Christian Ministry* will take its proper place in the contemporary literature on this

important topic, providing immediate help to many who need it
desperately.

Kenneth O. Gangel
Dallas, Texas
December 1988

Introduction

Evaluation of the church and its leaders is a precarious undertaking. Appraisal of the ancient church is readily accepted, but finding fault with the contemporary church strikes too close to home for modern comfort. Thus, historians confidently note the excesses of the church in the Middle Ages, but contemporary writers are hesitant to cite imperfections in the church at First and Main streets. Some Christians think any criticism of the church is unseemly. Of course, we must be sensitive to the fact that this is Christ's body and he said, "I will build my church, and the gates of Hades will not overcome it" (Matt. 16:18).

In spite of these caveats, it is necessary to assess past performance and suggest ways of improvement for the future. It is always hoped that critiques are constructive, tempered with charity, and seasoned with salt. True Christians love the church in spite of its flaws.

Having spent more than twenty years in pastoral ministry and eleven years teaching leadership in a theological seminary, I have great love for the church. Yet, I am deeply concerned. I have traveled a fair amount, observed a considerable number of congregations, and talked with scores of church leaders. My distinct impression is that not many churches are excellent models of harmony and effectiveness in ministry. More than a few are deeply troubled or mired in mediocrity.

Churches and their leaders are often anguished or indifferent, and the difficulties do not seem to be associated with any particular church polity or size. The troubles themselves are evident: interpersonal tension, schism, brief pastorates, leader burnout or dropout, laity disillusionment, status quo mentality, declining membership, upside-down priorities, and the unmet needs of people are indicators of spiritual impotency.

The causes are less clear than the crises and are inevitably complex. At the risk of being simplistic, I suggest that leadership is primarily responsible for church malfunction. No church achieves excellence in ministry without mature, capable leadership; excellent leadership generally produces effective churches. Jesus majored in leadership training during his earthly ministry. We would do well to follow his example.

Many congregations experience a continual power struggle with their leaders or among their leaders. There is considerable antagonism or uncertainty over the scriptural counsel to "obey your leaders and submit to their authority" (Heb. 13:17). Evidence suggests a growing resistance to leaders among members, probably with sufficient cause.

What authority church leaders should have or what constitutes the proper expression of that authority is not generally agreed upon. Abuse of power and position is not unusual. The whole church suffers from each breach of trust. When church members fail to respect their leaders, it is probably because leaders have failed to earn respect. If few are following, it is presumably because few are leading wisely and scripturally. If there is resistance to church leadership, misuse of leaders' prerogatives is likely to be found.

Leadership failure rarely occurs because of cognitive or theological defect. Rather, the deficiencies of leaders focus on inadequate relational skills, communication ability, motivational tactics, decision making, and use of authority. Weaknesses in these vital areas dramatize the serious flaws in traditional education for clergy preparing for local church ministry. Only in recent years have some ministerial training schools deemed the teaching of leadership essential. Lack of leadership training may still be the most glaring deficiency in the average seminarian's academic preparation.

Most church leaders have gained whatever leadership knowledge they have the hard way, through painful experience, through trial and error. Such experience is often an unforgiving teacher, and many are bruised along the way. Numerous good people quit ministry altogether. Lay leaders frequently bring a leadership style that has worked successfully in the business community, and they are shocked at its ineffectiveness in the church. They fail to understand that the church is a unique entity.

Leadership in the church has a twofold function, both elements equal in importance. One element focuses on *task*, fulfilling purposes, getting jobs done, and accomplishing goals. The other element focuses on *relationships*, maintaining fellowship, harmony, and cohesiveness within the body. It is destructive to favor one at the expense of the other. Good leaders assist the church to accomplish its worldwide mission *and* build a unified fellowship of believers.

We are constantly tempted to measure the effectiveness of leaders in materialistic terms (bodies, budgets, and buildings), but to do so is a tragic mistake. Rather, leaders and churches must be evaluated by two achievements: fulfilling the mission of the church (*task*), generally recognized to be meaningful worship, the edification of believers, the evangelization of the lost, and the meeting of a variety of real needs, *and* fostering the cohesiveness of the church (*relationships*), defined by fellowship in unity ("one accord") and *agape* (love) enjoined by Scripture.

These two primary objectives of spiritual leadership are interdependent and interrelated. Neither can be sacrificed on the altar of expediency. To achieve only one is to fail in a crucial dimension of biblical leadership. Moreover, it is doubtful whether one can truly be achieved without the other.

What kind of leader earns the respect of the congregation, preserves unity in the church, and accomplishes the church's task? There are no quick solutions or easy answers, but there is help and hope. Scripture and experience can lead us to an effective philosophy of leadership.

There is no substitute for sound judgment and common sense—

qualities that are difficult to teach. Some skills are acquired only by maturity and in-service training. Hence, an overseer "must not be a recent convert" (1 Tim. 3:6) and deacons "must first be tested" (1 Tim. 3:10). Academic achievement cannot substitute for seasoning.

There are inevitable differences of opinion, personality, and style. No one can respond perfectly to every conceivable circumstance. However, sensible guidelines can be developed and tested by Scripture and common sense so that, in the pressures of differing situations, leaders are able to grow in competence and effectiveness as they guide the church.

This book attempts to suggest such guidelines to all church leaders, not merely professional clergy. For this reason, the words *leaders* and *leadership* are used consistently and the words *pastor* and *clergy* are used sparingly. Obviously, however, leadership philosophy has a direct bearing upon clergy because their roles are so conspicuous and influential in the church. Failure in leadership brings the inevitable consequences of church stagnation, fragmentation, and deterioration. Effectiveness in leadership brings the joy of fruitful ministry and loving fellowship.

PART 1

Definition of Leadership in the Church

1

The Leadership of the Church

Churches need better leaders. Most churches have suffered the consequences of poor leadership at some point: conflict, stagnation, and impotency. Leadership exists to guide the church to spiritual vitality, unity, and effective ministry. When the purposes of the church are not fulfilled, leadership must accept primary responsibility.

Of course, there are times when the very best of Christian leaders cannot function constructively because of factors entirely beyond their control. Paul and the other early church leaders were not always successful in their leadership efforts, especially when evaluated by materialistic standards. Nevertheless, churches usually become reflections of their leadership. If churches are torn by disunity and become spiritually unproductive, we must look first to see if leadership has failed to function according to scriptural guidelines.

Many leaders are confused over what it means to "direct the affairs of the church" (1 Tim. 5:17). Some position themselves as

17

divinely sanctioned autocrats who "take charge" and "run the church." Others are only hired hands or syncophants who merely maintain the status quo or endeavor to gain a following by servility; they have negligible influence or authority and receive minimal respect. Still others fluctuate wildly between these extremes of leadership style without apparent reason or logic, desperately trying to find something pragmatically effective.

Many persons who hold spiritual office are of high integrity, intellect, and devotion, but simply do not know how to function as leaders in the contemporary church. The crisis of leadership deficiency may well be one of the most pervasive and pernicious problems facing contemporary Christianity.

Evidences of Leadership Crisis

There are a number of major indications that churches suffer from inadequate spiritual leadership as we near the end of the twentieth century. Five symptoms suggest deficient leadership in many churches.

Absence of Growth

A great number of churces fail to influence their communities, witness persuasively, and grow. Many churches exist decade after decade but never seem to have much impact. The average church in America has fewer than one hundred members. Poor leadership is not the sole cause of stagnation in these churches, but it is surely a significant factor in many of them.

Spiritual vitality or effectiveness of ministry should not be confused with church size. Some leaders (who often become celebrities) preside over spectacular numerical growth, but they sometimes fail in other, more crucial dimensions of ministry. It is possible that the megachurches do not meet God's ideal any more than do churches that have never grown. Yet, it is difficult to imagine a resourceful, witnessing, caring body of believers guided by competent leaders that fails to experience growth and to plant new churches, especially in metropolitan areas. God's intention is for the church to multiply itself, to "make disciples" in obedience to the Great Commission (Matt. 28:19).

No church, company, or organization becomes dynamic without adequate leadership. Thomas Peters and Robert Waterman emphasize this ingredient in successful business enterprises: "Associated with almost every excellent company was a strong leader (or two) who seemed to have had a lot to do with making the company excellent in the first place."[1] The same principle certainly is true for the church. It is a primary reason God demands such high qualifications for church leaders.

There are many reasons for church growth, and some of them are not directly associated with leadership, but perhaps the one common ingredient in all churches that experience healthy growth is competent leadership. Capable leaders infuse vision, motivation, direction, teaching, care, nurture, and inspiration to bring vitality and dynamism to the body. Absence of such leadership makes even the tiniest steps of progress extraordinarily difficult.

Discord

With alarming regularity congregations quibble, quarrel, and divide. Sometimes these divisions become overt, resulting in actual schism in the body. At other times, the dissension is contained and tolerated internally but never truly resolved. Many leaders are aware of individuals or groups permanently estranged from others in the church. Church leaders typically spend a disproportionate share of their time in conflict management, often with only limited success. Some churches have not heeded Paul's exhortation: "Make every effort to keep the unity of the Spirit through the bond of peace" (Eph. 4:3).

One of the primary tasks of leaders is to promote a spirit of cohesiveness and fellowship throughout the church. Church division or discord between any two individual members or families is injurious to the cause of Christ. Dissension frequently makes the church the target of sneers from outsiders. Whenever there is disunity in the church, leadership must examine itself to see where it has failed in its fundamental responsibility.

In Dallas, Texas, a church split when an elder felt slighted because he had received a smaller slice of ham at a church dinner than one sitting next to him.[2] This example surely is not typical. One suspects that there were other factors in the case that went

1. Thomas Peters and Robert Waterman, *In Search of Excellence* (New York: Warner, 1982), 26.
2. Reported by Dwight Pentecost in *The Joy of Living* (Grand Rapids: Zondervan, 1973), 55.

unreported. Yet, overwhelming evidence suggests that many
churches are torn by such pettiness, are crippled by interpersonal
tension, and suffer anguish because of internal turmoil. The issues
behind such troubles usually have nothing to do with major theological doctrines. The concerns are often trivial and frequently may
be traced to the leaders.

Discord and interpersonal conflict are as old as the church of
Corinth, but probably these problems have never been so conspicuous or destructive to the testimony and effectiveness of the
church in its community as it is in our day, partly because of the
media attention given to such cases. Excellent leadership does much
to promote cohesiveness and true Christian fellowship.

Brief Pastorates and Burnout

The average length of a pastoral ministry in the United States
is less than three years. There are undoubtedly many reasons for
this discouraging statistic. The brief tenure of the average pastoral
ministry is not always evidence of pastoral failure. Often the problem lies with laity leadership which does not function as God
intended. Sometimes a short pastorate has nothing to do with
leadership.

Conversely, some pastors behave inappropriately, particularly in
their leadership efforts, and bring trouble upon themselves. They
may be offensive in the pulpit, err in church business meetings,
become too aggressive in small groups or committees, use unwise
tactics, or fail in one-to-one relationships. People become alienated
and eventually, when enough people are dissatisfied, they effectively bring about an end to the pastor's ministry in the local church.

Whatever the reasons, pastoral resignations and firings are on
the increase. Nearly 7 percent of Southern Baptist ministers on
congregational staffs are fired annually by their churches.[3] Other
denominations probably have similarly depressing statistics. These
pastors are often bruised, battered, and disillusioned with ministry in the local church. Even when their personal integrity, devotion to Christ, and ministerial calling remain unquestioned, these
pastors often come to doubt the viability of pastoral ministry.

3. A statistic given by Brooks Faulkner, supervisor of the Southern Baptist career
guidance section, reported in the *Rocky Mountain News*, Denver, Col., April 28, 1984.

Another fact of pastoral life is burnout. "Burnout," writes John Sanford, "is a word we use when a person has become exhausted with his or her profession or life activity."[4] Many burned-out pastors hang on in the ministry, unable or unwilling to do otherwise, but restlessly move from church to church in apparent hope of finding an environment more conducive for ministry. R. M. Healey reported surveys that indicate many ministers are "leading lives of unquiet desperation."[5] Joseph Sittler coined the expression *the maceration of the minister* to describe what he saw in today's clergy.[6] Ministerial entropy, burnout, and dropping out decimate the church.

A study of pastors who sought consultation at the Menninger Foundation noted that one of the significant problems is

> a desperate groping for relevant religious faith. Pastors themselves are subject to so many demands from others that they begin to feel in need of a pastor themselves. Many experienced this as a gradual sense of losing the reality of the faith that they proclaimed, related to their own tendency to give up on really important central tasks in favor of becoming mere functionaries, playing their roles with decreasing involvement, commitment, and integrity.[7]

The reasons for brief pastoral ministries and burnout differ widely, and are sometimes complicated, but the fact that the typical church loses its pastors with remarkable regularity is compelling evidence that better leadership is needed throughout the church.

Spectator Religion

One of the major concerns of church leadership ought to be the dismal reality of spectator religion in modern society. Few things are so disconcerting as the numbers of professing Christians who are spiritually dysfunctional.

Nobody knows how many *former* church members there are, but the number must be large. Most church leaders could assemble a list of people who were once involved, but frustration with church power structures, leaders, boards, and the decision-making pro-

4. John Sanford, *Ministry Burnout* (New York: Paulist, 1982), 1.
5. R. M. Healey, "The Ministerial Mystique," *The Christian Century* 91 (1974): 121–25.
6. Ibid., 122.
7. Donald C. Houts, "Pastoral Care for Pastors: Toward a Church Strategy," *Pastoral Psychology* 25 (Spring 1977): 186–96.

cess (and other reasons) provoke members to give up on the church. Some of these people become active in another local church. Sometimes they become vagabonds, drifting from church to church. Frequently they drop out of the church altogether or become enamored of the media church. Others gravitate to the pews of large churches where they are entertained by performers in an atmosphere very much like that of a Hollywood studio. Many of these professing Christians become mere attendants in a contemporary brand of pseudo-Christianity. Some churches cater to this spectator mentality.

Surely one of the saddest realities haunting the modern church is that of spectator Christians. Leadership has a major role to play in rekindling the spiritual vitality of this enormous resource. The spectator syndrome of modern religion requires leaders to provide the kind of leadership that halts the exodus and reenlists the onlookers.

Nonministering Churches

Genuine ministry is functionally crippled or nonexistent in many churches. Churches that are neither salt nor light in their communities dot the landscape. They may have beautiful buildings and impressive statistics, but they are spiritually stagnant—sad testimonies to another era. They have become anachronisms.

Numerous churches in every major city carry on feverish activity of all kinds, but have little that qualifies as authentic ministry. Many churches have no meaningful evangelistic outreach in their communities; outreach is relegated to a committee whose primary concern is sending dollars overseas. They lack true discipleship ministry.

Genuine ministry involves comforting the bereaved, caring for the sick, disciplining the wayward, feeding the hungry, erecting support structures for the poor, preaching the Word, encouraging the aged, healing the wounded, strengthening the weak, sheltering the homeless, equipping the saints, developing spiritual gifts, and sending missionaries. Many churches conduct services and run programs that never touch these needs.

It is the responsibility of leadership to direct the church to spiritual health, meaningful worship, and vigorous ministry in its community. If the church is weak and has lost its sense of purpose, leadership must accept the responsibility. Robert A. Raines is correct: "That the average church member and the typical local church have lost their sense of mission is ultimately a judgment upon us who are leaders of the church."[8]

Leadership influences people and shapes institutions. The results of church ministry greatly depend on the quality of the leaders and the appropriateness of their conduct. The very fact that we have so many weak churches and relatively few examples of vibrant, ministering churches testifies that better leadership is needed in the local church. The spiritual anemia of so many Protestant churches indicates a leadership crisis. James Burns, who wrote a modern classic on leadership, suggested that "one of the most universal cravings of our time is a hunger for compelling and creative leadership."[9] That surely is true in the church.

A distinguished professor of business administration at the University of Southern California, Warren Bennis, said, "Instead of leaders, we have celebrities, stars, heroes."[10] While he was speaking of our world and not of the church, one suspects that his words are equally applicable to our contemporary religious scene.

Who Are the Leaders?

Formal church leadership is usually categorized as either professional or nonprofessional. Professional church leaders are generally called clergy.[11] Clergy normally have some higher educational training in ministry, are formally ordained to ministry by the church, and earn their living from their ministry. Other church leaders are called lay leaders.

Clergy usually take too much blame for church failure and too much credit for church success. On the other hand, the importance and effectiveness of lay leadership is underestimated in our society, but it is encouraging to note a revived emphasis upon the contributions of lay leadership, at least in some denominations. A few groups have made significant strides in equipping the laity and

8. Robert A. Raines, *New Life in the Church* (New York: Harper and Row, 1961), 15.

9. James Burns, *Leadership* (New York: Harper and Row, 1979), 1.

10. In an address delivered at the Leadership Education Conference, Center for Creative Leadership, Greensboro, N.C., July 22, 1987.

11. Of course, some churches have professionals on their staffs who are not clergy, such as secretaries, administrative assistants, or bookkeepers. Their skills are secular, not ministerial, gifts.

entrusting them with responsibility. Current, popular books on ecclesiology argue for multiple spiritual leaders with shared responsibility in the church. Today's theologians point out that a plurality of leaders seems to have been the norm for New Testament churches.

Modern thinking also tends to erase or downplay some of the historical distinctions between clergy and laity. Some believe this tendency has gone too far, but the polarization of the church into clergy and laity cannot be supported by the usage of these terms in the New Testament.[12] Clergy should not be thought of as a separate, ruling caste over the church, nor should laity be thought of as an inferior class of church member.

The Greek word *laos* (people), from which we get our English noun *laity*, is never used in the New Testament to distinguish between professional staff and other church members.[13] J. B. Lightfoot observed: "All Christians are God's laity (*laos*) and all are God's clergy (*kleroi*)."[14] Elton Trueblood asserted that "the conventional modern distinction between the clergy and laity simply does not occur in the New Testament at all."[15] Until postapostolic times, clergy and laity were not classified separately.[16] Although distinctions between clergy and laity are not clearly drawn in the New Testament, there are some obvious differences among various positions of responsibility, gifts, and callings.

Since our concern is with a philosophy of leadership and leadership behavior, we will forego a lengthy exposition of the formal titles and offices themselves. Other writers have expounded clearly

12. See Robert Saucy, *The Church in God's Program* (Chicago: Moody, 1972); Larry Richards and Clyde Hoeldtke, *A Theology of Church Leadership* (Grand Rapids: Zondervan, 1980); John Moore and Ken Neff, *A New Testament Blueprint for the Church* (Chicago: Moody, 1985); and many others.

13. *Laos,* in the sense of "God's people," is found in Acts 15:14; 18:10; Romans 9:25–26; 2 Corinthians 6:16; Titus 2:14; 1 Peter 2:9–10; Hebrews 4:9; 8:10; 10:30; 13:12; Revelation 18:4; 21:3.

14. J. B. Lightfoot, *The Christian Ministry* (New York: Macmillan, 1901), 20.

15. Elton Trueblood, *The Incendiary Fellowship* (New York: Harper and Row, 1967), 39.

16. For the use of *kleroi* see Gerhard Kittel, ed., *Theological Dictionary of the New Testament* (Grand Rapids: Eerdmans, 1964), 3:758–59. For an explanation of the development of clerical superiority see H. Richard Niebuhr, *The Purpose of the Church and Its Ministry* (New York: Harper and Brothers, 1956), 28–29.

the relevant passages in considerable detail.[17] The conduct and authority of church leadership, whether professional and or non-professional, is our area of interest. The New Testament seems to identify only two formal official positions in the church (e.g., Phil. 1:1). A brief examination of these will be sufficient.

Elders

The biblical terms *overseer, elder,* and *pastor* are generally used interchangeably in the New Testament and refer to the spiritual leader(s) primarily responsible for preaching-teaching, shepherding, and presiding. Current thinking is that elders may be either clergy or nonclergy. Many contemporary churches have both clergy and laity forming a board of elders that directs the day-to-day affairs of the church with varying degrees of authority and responsibility. Some churches allow women to be elders or pastors; others believe that Scripture precludes women from these offices.

The term *overseer* (or, *bishop*; Greek *episkopos*) may be more closely associated with Greek culture, while the term *elder* (Greek *presbuteros*) seems more Jewish. *Elder* appears to be primarily a title; *overseer* refers to an office; and *pastor* (Greek *poimanos*) designates the shepherding functions of that office. Multiple leadership, a plurality of elders, was the norm of New Testament churches, if not the imperative of Scripture. However, as in many things, the Bible is more descriptive than prescriptive on this point.

It has become increasingly popular in our day to elect or otherwise choose a plurality of elders, and it is difficult to fault this practice. Sometimes these officers have significant governmental power. This is frequently called the elder-rule form of church government, though *elder rule* is often a misnomer that has caused confusion and dissension, particularly in ecclesiastical traditions that have stressed congregational authority.

Some church traditions have had elder rule for centuries, but recently a number of churches that traditionally have been congregational in government have adjusted their organizational structure to accommodate the concept of multiple elders. The emergence of

17. Saucy, *The Church in God's Program*; F. F. Bruce, *The Acts of the Apostles* (Philadelphia: Inter-Varsity Christian Fellowship, 1952); W. T. Purkiser, *The New Testament Image of the Ministry* (Grand Rapids: Baker, 1970); John R. W. Stott, *The Preacher's Portrait* (Grand Rapids: Eerdmans, 1961); and others.

elder boards in these churches has caused considerable controversy. The controversy focuses on how much authority elders should
have in the church and how much authority the congregation itself
should retain. In other words, the issue is control over the decision-
making process.

That it is appropriate, maybe even necessary, to have more than
one elder, according to the size or needs of the congregation, is
indisputable. Each time the term *elder* appears in the New Testament it appears in the plural form. Paul and Barnabas ordained
"elders in every church" (Acts 14:23; cf. Titus 1:5).

The expression *elder rule* often conveys the objectionable impression that the elders are to have nearly complete (or, in some cases,
total) legislative or decision-making power over the congregation.
Such a definition of responsibility is difficult or impossible to de-
fend scripturally. For example, the penultimate step in church discipline involves taking the matter to the church body for its action
(Matt. 18:17), not to the elders of the church. In Acts 15 the representatives of the church at Antioch reported to the church at
Jerusalem, not merely to the apostles and elders. The church certainly participated in the decision-making process and "then the
apostles and elders, *with the whole church* [italics added], decided
to choose some of their own men and send them to Antioch with
Paul and Barnabas" (Acts 15:22).[18] Other examples demonstrate
how the New Testament church participated in significant decisions, serving as a model for the modern church.

The problem lies in the definition of elder authority, or in the
perception of that authority. Our English word *rule,* for example,
connotes a far greater legislative or controlling power than did its
biblical counterparts.[19]

Some churches have embraced the concept of elder rule to the
extent of having a self-perpetuating elder board. This structure
denies the congregation participation in the selection of its own
leaders and is difficult to support scripturally, although there are
those who try, sometimes on the grounds that the apostles often
appointed elders (Acts 14:23).

There is evidence in the New Testament that elders did not have

18. See chapter 12 for a discussion of decision making in Acts 15.
19. Greek *proistēmi,* literally "to stand before," hence, "to lead, attend to," as in
Romans 12:8; 1 Timothy 3:4, 5, 12; 5:17; or Greek *hegēomai,* "to lead," as in Hebrews
13:17, 24. Both Greek words are sometimes translated "rule."

the governmental power that is frequently assigned to them today, although the apostles often exerted a commanding authority.[20] Those who argue for a strong, authoritarian elder board usually point to Paul's example.[21] However, we must remember that Paul was an apostle writing under supernatural inspiration, and even then his authority rested firmly in the authority of Christ, the head of the church.[22] Most church polities today deny their elders apostolic authority over the church except in their proclamation of unequivocally clear scriptural teaching, in which case the authority is that of the Word of God, not the elders. This question of leadership authority will be thoroughly discussed later in this book.

To many theologians and traditions it seems advisable for congregations to retain control over significant matters (e.g., the selection of leaders, excommunication of church members, the acceptance of sizable debt, and adoption of annual budgets) and to delegate most other matters to leaders. However, the many diverse church polities see this issue differently, and it is not the purpose of this book to argue for a particular form of church government.

The important thing is that Scripture does not emphasize the rights, privileges, and authority of the church's elders; rather, Scripture emphasizes the qualifications, responsibilities, and obligations of spiritual leaders. Failure to note this has caused much dissent over appropriate leadership authority. Although the Bible does not specifically say how much authority church leaders should have, it explicitly opposes attitudes of demagoguery in the church.

The duties of elders are to shepherd the flock of God and be spiritual models for others to follow (1 Pet. 5:2–3); to exercise spiritual oversight (Acts 20:28); to equip the saints for their own ministries (Eph. 4:11–12); to preside over and guide the church (1 Tim. 5:17); and to exhort and encourage by sound doctrine (Titus 1:9). Further, scholars tend to agree that the division of elders into ruling elders and teaching elders does not seem warranted by 1 Timothy 5:17.

No single selection process for elders is prescribed or mandated

20. For example, "We have confidence in the Lord that you are doing and will continue to do the things we command" (2 Thess. 3:4).

21. Note numerous passages in the Corinthian letters.

22. "You know what instructions we gave you by the authority of the Lord Jesus" (1 Thess. 4:2).

in Scripture. Some scholars conclude that election by the church is inherent in the Greek word translated "appoint" (Acts 14:23; 2 Cor. 8:19 RSV).[23] Paul referred to the elders at Ephesus as those holding office by the action of the Holy Spirit (Acts 20:28). In any case, a careful consideration of the necessary qualifications is commanded (1 Tim. 3:10; 5:22).

Deacons

The other main office in the church referred to in the New Testament is that of deacon. There is relatively little controversy in the contemporary church with regard to the function of deacons. Their responsibility is clearly ministerial and administrative, as is indicated by the word *deacon* (Greek *diakonos*, minister, servant).[24] Deacons were appointed for the express purpose of allowing the apostles more time for the ministry of the Word and for prayer (see Acts 6).[25] Early deacons assumed certain administrative responsibilities in the body of believers. Clearly, the early apostles and elders of the church felt that it was not right to allow themselves to be unduly burdened with the daily responsibilities of waiting on tables. These tasks, though important, conflicted with other responsibilities of higher priority for the elders.

Many churches holding to a congregational polity have not had lay elders working closely with their clergy, although the current trend is in that direction. Instead, in these churches the most influential lay leadership has been provided by deacons who have been given administrative, managerial, and ministerial responsibilities under congregational authority. In other words, some churches have traditionally given deacons the same status and responsibilities that other churches have assigned to elders.

The earliest deacons apparently were selected by the church; there is little evidence to suggest that they were appointed by the elders or apostles, although in some cases this may have been done. Scripture does not explicitly state a means of selection.

23. Bruce, *The Acts of the Apostles*; Douglas Bannerman, *The Scripture Doctrine of the Church* (Grand Rapids: Baker, 1976).

24. This is not to infer that the function of elders is not ministerial, but to indicate a different *kind* of ministry.

25. Nowhere in Acts 6 are the seven chosen men called deacons, although they are generally recognized as the prototype of the diaconate.

Other Leaders

In addition to these formal church offices there are other positions of formal or informal leadership. Some theologians, such as John Calvin, differentiate between clergy (or pastors) and elders, suggesting that the ordination of the clergy and their special tasks of preaching, teaching, and administering the ordinances or sacraments mark them as holders of an office different from that of elder. Others suggest that apostle, prophet, and evangelist should be recognized as contemporary church offices (Eph. 4:11). It is not necessary here to debate these differing interpretations. We simply need to recognize that elders and deacons obviously were leaders of the church (Phil. 1:1; 1 Tim. 3) and that the word *pastor* apparently is used interchangeably with *elder* or *bishop*. Certainly there were other leaders; whether their positions should be recognized as offices is questionable.

Anyone who has responsibility and influence could be considered a leader, since leadership is defined not by positions held, but by followers influenced. Highly respected Sunday school teachers, though not elders or deacons, may be considered strong leaders because of their powerful influence in the lives of many people. Conversely, an elected elder or deacon who is not respected and not followed could hardly be thought of as a leader, in spite of the office held.

Formal office holders are not always the most influential leaders. Rather, Sunday school teachers, prominent citizens, retired office holders, former pastors, outspoken members, generous givers, members of ad hoc committees, charter members, dearly loved saints, or secular employers of members sometimes have power in a local church. In this context, the behavior of all leaders—elected or appointed, professional or lay, officer or not—is significant because every leader has impact upon followers and the church body.

Although the greatest influence does not always rest with those in formal positions, influence tends to be strongly associated with one's perceived reputation. Those who are most loved and respected usually have the most power. Sometimes, however, there are those who have great power not because they are respected or loved, but because they are feared or because they intimidate others. The current problems of church leadership center on the nature of leadership and the exercise of authority.

Summary

The church urgently needs better leaders. Little growth, dissension, brief pastorates, leader burnout, spectator religion, and non-ministering churches are facts in modern Christianity that both reveal deficiency in leadership and call for greater excellence in leadership. There are many other important considerations in modern church life, but certainly better leadership would have a profound impact upon the unpleasant and discouraging elements in the contemporary church.

Formal church leaders are those elected or appointed to official positions. Professional church leaders are generally referred to as clergy, and nonprofessional leaders are designated laity. This division frequently seems arbitrary and difficult to support by the New Testament. In addition, there may be professional church leaders who are not clergy.

Two church offices commonly are recognized in the church and are mentioned in the New Testament: the office of overseer, elder, or pastor (the terms usually are used interchangeably) and the office of deacon. Elders may be either clergy or laity, in the opinion of many biblical scholars. There usually are numerous other leaders in the church; some church traditions recognize additional officers, or designate their officers by different titles.

Anyone who influences the lives of other church members or the decision-making process may be thought of as a leader, whether or not there is popular recognition of the fact. Informal, nonelected, or nonappointed leaders are often the most powerful people in the church. Power is associated with perceived reputation, but a person may accumulate power by other (sometimes questionable) means.

The nature of spiritual leadership and the exercise of its authority form the focal points of the current leadership crisis.

2

The Imperative of Leadership
Reputation

Research in the field of leadership is confusing, ambiguous, and, frequently, contradictory. Hence, the study of leadership can be a frustrating endeavor. Ralph Stogdill exhaustively surveyed the voluminous research on leadership and concluded, "It is difficult to know what, if anything, has been convincingly demonstrated by replicated research. The endless accumulation of empirical data has not produced an integrated understanding of leadership."[1] Michael Lombardo and Morgan McCall, Jr., concluded that students of leadership have discovered "1) [t]he number of unintegrated models, theories, prescriptions, and conceptual schemes of leadership is mind-boggling; 2) [m]uch of the literature is fragmentary, trivial, unrealistic, or dull; and 3) [t]he research results are characterized by Type III errors (solving the wrong problem precisely) and by contradictions."[2]

1. Ralph Stogdill, *Handbook of Leadership* (New York: Free Press, 1974), vii.
2. Morgan McCall, Jr., and Michael Lombardo, eds., *Leadership: Where Else Can We Go?* (Durham, N.C.: Duke University Press, 1978), 3.

In the light of such damaging admissions, how can we gener-
alize, much less specify, the essential requirements for effective
church leaders?

Despite the mass of confusing data, the most conspicuous and
proven fact is that effective leadership depends upon integrity, the
leader's character as perceived by followers. Aristotle called this
ethos, the credit rating or perception of character, the first and
most important of the available means of persuasion. Without a
reputation for integrity and trustworthiness, a leader cannot truly
be effective anywhere, especially in the church. The leader must
be deemed worth following.

The Bible describes in detail the impeccable personal characteristics necessary for spiritual leadership. God knew from the beginning what some people are just now discovering: Unless leaders
are perceived to be people of outstanding integrity they cannot
lead for long. If they lack integrity, leaders will be revealed eventually for what they really are: manipulators, power grabbers, or
exploiters. They will be rejected by followers. Followers insist upon
integrity. There are those who seem to defy this rule for a time,
but inevitably their power over followers degenerates to some form
of coercion; it is not genuine leadership.

Leadership Qualifications

The church needs to return to biblical teaching regarding leadership qualifications. The primary passages are in 1 Timothy and
Titus. Although Paul refers specifically to elders and deacons, the
broad, applicable truth is that quite stringent limitations are put
on the selection of the church's spiritual leaders, regardless of office
held. The qualifications for elder and deacon are not significantly
different. If God were to give us a list of qualifications for other
positions of spiritual leadership, he would undoubtedly use basically the same list.

The foundational truth is that spiritual leaders "must be above
reproach. . . . [The overseer] must also have a good reputation
with outsiders, so that he will not fall into disgrace and into the
devil's trap" (1 Tim. 3:2, 7). Integrity—soundness of moral principle and character, uprightness, and honesty—is the essential
characteristic for effective spiritual leadership. One who lacks in-

tegrity is not to be selected for leadership and invested with its authority and responsibility. Moreover, leaders are to conduct themselves in such a manner that they are perceived as blameless by the community in which they serve. No one is able to successfully lodge a charge against one who is above reproach.

Personal integrity and a Christian example that people in the community can respect were identified as two of the top three characteristics for effective leadership in the church, according to an extensive research project of the Association of Theological Schools.[3] This certainly harmonizes with scriptural injunction.

Parenthetically, it is interesting to note that the business community has come to recognize the validity of this same quality: "This component is your 'credit rating' with other people as to your integrity, reliability, honesty, loyalty, sincerity, personal morals, and ethics. Obviously you will get more and better action from a man who has respect for your character than from one who hasn't."[4]

The passages in 1 Timothy and Titus detail what it means to be blameless and above reproach. The lengthy list of qualities is synthesized here under a few categories. These traits seem to be regarded in Scripture as inherent in integrity. No order of importance is attached.

Spirituality

The church leader must be spiritually authentic and alive, in touch with God, disciplined in personal habits of devotion. Few things are so destructive in the church as leaders who are spiritual frauds, wolves in sheep's clothing (Matt. 7:15). Perhaps Paul's most basic and important counsel is contained in his first letter to Timothy:

> [T]rain yourself to be godly. . . . [g]odliness has value for all things, holding promise for both the present life and the life to come. . . . [S]et an example for the believers in speech, in life, in love, in faith and in purity. . . . Be diligent in these matters; give yourself wholly to them, so that everyone may see your progress. [4:7–8, 12, 15]

3. David S. Schuller, Milo L. Brekke, and Merton P. Strommen, *Readiness for Ministry* (Vandalia, Ohio: The Association of Theological Schools in the United States and Canada, 1975), 1:6.
4. William Oncken, Jr., "The Authority to Manage," quoted by Ted W. Engstrom in *The Making of a Christian Leader* (Grand Rapids: Zondervan, 1976), 113.

Charles Spurgeon said, "An ill life will effectually drown the voice of the most eloquent ministry." Through the scandals in the lives of prominent Christian leaders in recent years, we have been reminded just how true Spurgeon's words are. The leader must "watch [his] life and doctrine closely . . . [and] pursue righteousness, godliness, faith, love, endurance and gentleness" (1 Tim. 4:16; 6:11).

Leaders must know God and live under the discipline of the Word of God and the Spirit of God. John Harris wrote, "The personal authenticity of the minister . . . is the greatest strength of any congregation. The inauthenticity of the clergy is the greatest weakness of organized religion."[5] Of course, the truth is as applicable to lay leaders as to professional clergy.

Maturity

Emotional and spiritual stability are prerequisites to effective leadership. Paul admonished, "He [the leader] must not be a recent convert, or he may become conceited and fall under the same judgment as the devil" (1 Tim. 3:6); and "do not be hasty in the laying on of hands" (1 Tim. 5:22). The New Testament concept of the elder in particular borrows heavily from the Jewish Old Testament perspective that one achieves maturity and wisdom with the accumulated years. Maturity, of course, is not always related to chronological age. Some people never mature; others mature at a surprisingly young age.

Maturity is necessary if a leader is to react properly to criticism, manage time carefully, be disciplined in work habits, behave appropriately and with common sense in a variety of situations, counsel with godly wisdom, be self-controlled, be gentle, be not quarrelsome, and so forth.

Congeniality

Church leaders promote Christian fellowship and brotherly love and therefore must be hospitable, friendly, companionable. The extraordinary degree of affection displayed between the apostle Paul and the churches is obvious. Paul either was extraordinarily gifted or worked very hard at building significant relationships. He put a premium on his relationships with people.

5. John Harris, *Stress, Power and Ministry* (Washington, D.C.: Alban Institute, 1979), 3.

People who are consistently abrasive, aloof, or unsociable are unable to develop the trust and affection that are necessary to enduring leadership in the church. Sustained relationships marked by warmth and trust make continued ministry both possible and effectual.

Of course, leaders are not to be "menpleasers" (Col. 3:22 KJV); the Pharisees "loved praise from men more than praise from God" (John 12:43). Leaders must not sacrifice fundamental convictions or compromise theological necessities to win friendship. Yet, if leaders fail to develop affectionate, meaningful, transparent relationships within their congregations, they cannot serve effectively for long. Building bonds of mutual affection is essential to leadership in the church. Failure of pastors and church members to establish relationships of collegiality, or the deterioration of those relationships, results in short pastorates.

This does not mean that every leader must be extroverted or gregarious. Some effective leaders are reserved personalities, more at home in the world of books than in social settings, but they are nonetheless able to build trust and affection among their followers.

Compassion

Scripture requires church leaders to have tender hearts and care for the holistic well-being of people. Lack of compassion for people disqualifies one from spiritual leadership. The best leaders care profoundly for people of all kinds and all conditions. Nothing is so repugnant as church officers who have no real empathy with hurting people. When asked why he was preparing for the pastorate, one student replied: "It looks like a pretty good racket to me." Contrast that with Paul's touching testimony regarding Timothy: "I have no one else like him, who takes a genuine interest in your welfare" (Phil. 2:20).

Good leaders "rejoice with those who rejoice and mourn with those who mourn" (Rom. 12:15), not merely because they are commanded to do so, but because they genuinely care; God has given them a shepherd's heart. Servant-leaders are sensitive to people's needs, wants, feelings, temptations, struggles, and hurts. They are empathetic, as Cyril J. Barber and Gary H. Strauss state:

> We believe that the servant leader is sensitive to people. He seeks to understand how they think and feel, for this is the key to their

well-being. He, therefore, learns to listen. . . . [There is] an uncon-
ditional acceptance of others. . . . He treats people as people regardless of their performance. . . . [A]cceptance of a person requires
toleration of their imperfections and the patient, persistent development of all that is worthwhile in them.[6]

All of this defines servant-leadership and is crucial to both the
reputation and the effectiveness of a leader. Our attitude must be
the same as that of Christ, who took the very nature of a servant
and taught: "The good shepherd lays down his life for the sheep.
The hired hand is not the shepherd. . . . [He] runs away because
he is a hired hand and cares nothing for the sheep" (John 10:11–13).

Paul counseled, "Do nothing out of selfish ambition or vain con-
ceit, but in humility consider others better than yourselves. Each
of you should look not only to your own interests, but also to the
interests of others" (Phil. 2:3–4).

Without genuine compassion leaders cannot know their followers. They cannot be sensitive to their heartbeat, their hopes, desires, dreams. Without sympathetic understanding leaders cease
to be leaders; they become drivers or manipulators, committed,
perhaps, to achieving many goals, but not dedicated to the task of
serving the church in the self-sacrificing way in which Christ laid
down his life (1 John 3:16).

Effective leadership, genuine ministry, and church harmony all
begin in the leadership selection process. If the church chooses
mature, godly, compassionate, and gracious leaders, effective ministry and healthy growth are likely. If people who are not qualified
are chosen to be leaders, the church cannot fulfill God's purpose
for it in the community.

Failure to adhere to the biblical guidelines for leadership selection has severely crippled church ministry. We simply must honor
what God underscored. Personal and spiritual integrity, and the
public perception of it, form the irreducible minimum for effective
leadership in the church. Without these things no one can effectively lead the church.

Those aspiring to positions of leadership must focus not merely
on cognitive subjects and practical skills, but, more importantly,
upon spiritual integrity.

6. Cyril J. Barber, and Gary H. Strauss, *Leadership: The Dynamics of Success* (Greenwood, S.C.: Attic, 1982), 109–10.

Leadership Reputation in the Church

Leaders of the church have always struggled to achieve and maintain an excellent reputation among those they have served. In the earliest days of the church its leaders were often falsely accused and maligned.[7] The entire epistle of 2 Corinthians is largely a defense of Paul's reputation and ministry as an apostle.

Despite the scriptural admonitions to give elders "double honor" (1 Tim. 5:17), to "respect those who work hard among you" (1 Thess. 5:12), and to "hold them in the highest regard in love because of their work" (1 Thess. 5:13), esteem for the church's leaders has been steadily declining throughout the twentieth century. Speaking primarily of clergy, W. T. Purkiser stated, "In no other period since the Reformation has the popular appraisal of the work of the minister altered so drastically as in the last half-century."[8] The alteration is not flattering.

The deterioration of image (especially that of the clergy) was noted by Richard LaPiere: "A hundred years ago the Protestant ministry was a profession of high prestige and equally high morale. . . . Today the ministry is a profession as low in prestige as in income, and the general level of morale among ministers is lower still."[9] Church leaders have seldom been thought of with such disregard or downright contempt by the public at large and by the church's own constituency.

Why has there been a precipitous decline in leadership reputation in recent decades? A number of significant factors may be suggested.

Rejection of Authority

Respect for and deference to authority, so evident a century ago, have deteriorated throughout many parts of society. This challenge and rejection of authority accelerated tremendously (perhaps, peaked) in the late 1960s and early 1970s.

Societal problems with authority have undoubtedly contributed to the erosion of esteem for church leaders. Many, who in the past would have deferred to spiritual leaders, feel comfortable in de-

7. Note 2 Corinthians 10:1; 10:10; 13:3; and other texts.
8. W. T. Purkiser, *The New Testament Image of the Ministry* (Grand Rapids: Baker, 1970), 11.
9. Richard LaPiere, *Theory of Social Control* (New York: McGraw-Hill, 1954), vi.

bating and disputing with leaders. In other times, the authority of these leaders might have gone unchallenged, but not so today. Of course, there were times in the past when deference to church leaders was mindless. The pendulum has swung dramatically in the opposite direction.

Increased Educational Level

The increased educational level of church members has removed church leaders, particularly clergy, from the lofty pedestal they once enjoyed. At one time, church leaders were the most educated and respected citizens of the community, and the major collegiate schools existed to train them. That is not true today.

Not many decades ago the average church member was poorly educated. Deference to leaders who were highly educated was natural. This has changed significantly. With the rise of the overall educational level of congregations, there has come an increased demand for participation in church decision making and a resistance to leadership authority, particularly to those who abuse their authority.

Blind obeisance to religious authority figures is a thing of the past, except in certain sects that idolize gurus. That is undoubtedly healthy for the church, but it is also a challenge for church officers to be worthy of their positions of leadership.

Media Publicity

Since about the 1920s the media have increasingly exposed failures of religious leadership. Cults, mail-order ordinations, cheap degrees, and prominent, fallen leaders have been noted widely in the media. This has contributed to the erosion of leadership reputation. Never has the enemy within been so exposed as it is in our day. When a celebrated leader's conduct is less than exemplary, the world takes note, laughs, and eventually scorns.

Media detail the ugly stories of pastors convicted of criminal fraud, lay leaders embezzling church funds, court suits over church property, and the so-called Holy Wars.[10] These scandals of the church were once dealt with quietly, behind closed doors, and without publicity. This is not the case today.

10. As this is being written the media are detailing the unbecoming conduct of the leaders of several prominent ministries.

Skeletons in the church's closet have become front-page news. When a well-known Christian leader recently admitted to moral transgression, it was reported on virtually every radio and television station in this country (including religious stations) and it became the cover story in both *Time* and *Newsweek*. It is no surprise that the church and its leaders everywhere have lost esteem. We may consider it unfair for the reputation of all church leaders to suffer because of the serious transgressions of a few, but we must recognize this reality nonetheless.

Secularization of the Church

The modern mentality views the local church as a big (or little) enterprise, not significantly different from a business venture. In this view church leaders think of the church only in terms of ever-increasing profits, namely, human bodies enrolled and bigger budgets met.

This secularism has become pervasive in, even catastrophic to, the church. In describing the typical ministerial style, H. Richard Niebuhr refers to the pastor as the "big operator": "He is active in many affairs, organizes many societies, advertises the increases in membership and budget achieved under his administration and, in general, manages church business as if it were akin to the activities of a chamber of commerce."[11] One cannot help but wince at such a description of church leadership and wonder at the profound impact such secularization has had on leader-follower relations, leader reputation, and church ministry. Christian leadership that is oriented toward materialistic concerns, and also is spiritually poverty-stricken, suffers loss of integrity and reputation.

Materialistic concerns for increases in membership, profit-and-loss statements, and splendid, multimillion-dollar buildings have contributed to transforming its leaders into caricatures of biblical leadership. Sometimes it appears that this pervasive, secularistic attitude arises from the fleshly desires of leaders for the power and prestige that attend materialistic success. Yet, the members of the church often demand statistical impressiveness as the infallible sign of ministerial effectiveness. Sometimes church members unwittingly push their spiritual leaders to major in statistical productivity rather than effective ministry.

11. H. Richard Niebuhr, *The Purpose of the Church and Its Ministry* (New York: Harper and Brothers, 1956), 81.

Few things have so eroded esteem for church leaders as the secularization of the church. Church leaders are rarely viewed today as saints in touch with God, skilled in spiritual direction, but as managers, public-relations specialists, or administrators.

Many churches looking for leaders put a priority not upon godliness and ability in teaching, preaching, and discipling, but upon a wide range of secular skills (public relations, fund raising, organization, management, and programing). These abilities may be helpful, and sometimes even necessary, but they ought never to substitute for higher objectives. The church is not a business that needs better managers, but a living organism that needs better spiritual shepherds, leaders in the biblical sense of the word.

New Testament leaders were concerned with evangelism, discipleship, circumspect behavior, shepherding, and unity in the church. Departure from this biblical standard has cost the modern church dearly. "When secularism enters the church," observes Donald G. Bloesch, "the situation becomes critical, for it means the almost certain demise of traditional Christian values and concerns."[12]

Lack of Shepherding

Closely related to the secularization of the church and its leadership is the fact that shepherding has been deemphasized in favor of administrative efforts, slick performances, program management, recruitment of personnel, building budgets, and the like. To our shame and hurt, spiritual gifts and the transforming power of God have been displaced.

Deep within the church, but often unverbalized, is a fundamental hunger for leaders who obviously know God and know how to pray, preach, teach, disciple, equip, and shepherd. Many local churches do not feel that they have this kind of leadership, yet, they unwittingly have contributed to the problem. As a result, leadership is not respected: "Much of the research on ministry done in the last twenty-five years points to one conclusion: clergy are no longer equipped with the reliable, theoretical models of their craft, that is, those practical tools for preaching, spiritual guidance, congregational leadership, and pastoral care."[13]

12. Donald G. Bloesch, *Crumbling Foundations* (Grand Rapids: Zondervan, 1984), 39.
13. John Harris, *Stress, Power, and Ministry* (Washington, D.C.: Alban Institute, 1979), 59.

Shepherding used to be central to ministry; now it is considered "a fringe activity for most of us. Being a spiritual director, which used to loom large at the center of every pastor's common work, has been pushed in our times to the periphery of ministry."[14] Although these comments are directed specifically to clergy, they are clearly applicable to all church leaders.

When church leadership is regarded as bureaucratic management rather than spiritual direction, the credibility of leaders suffers irreparable damage. People resent being manipulated and managed as mere cogs in an organization. John R. W. Stott is absolutely correct:

> Herein also lies the peril of seeing leadership in terms of projects and programs. People must take precedence over projects. And people must be neither "manipulated" nor even "managed." Though the latter is less demeaning than the former, both words are derived from *manus,* meaning *hand,* and expressing a "handling" of people as if they were commodities rather than persons.[15]

Church leaders must not settle for the adulation accorded to those producing notable materialistic progress. Rather, church leaders must conduct themselves as godly, spiritual shepherds worthy of "double honor" and esteem in the church and community. Church leaders must gain esteem not by bureaucratic superiority, but by excellence in spiritual direction.

Only when leaders are recognized as godly shepherds will there be the trust that is indispensable to God's plan for the church. An aspiring junior partner asked how to win trust, and a wise senior executive responded wryly, "Try being trustworthy." Trustworthy church leaders are spiritual shepherds; spiritual shepherds are notably trustworthy.

Summary

Despite the ambiguity and confusion in leadership research, it is clear that spiritual leaders must be above reproach, possess per-

14. Eugene Peterson, "The Inglorious Work of Spiritual Direction," *Leadership* (Winter 1986): 51.
15. John R. W. Stott, "What Makes Leadership Christian?" *Christianity Today* (August 9, 1985): 26.

sonal integrity, and have a reputation for honorable character. Church leaders have always struggled to achieve and maintain the ethos necessary for effective leadership.

The church must return to a primary emphasis on the scriptural qualifications for spiritual leadership. Leaders who are spiritually authentic, blameless, mature, congenial, and compassionate must be recruited, trained, appointed, and invested with proper authority. Without leaders characterized by spiritual and personal integrity, true, enduring effectiveness is impossible in the church.

Leadership credibility has steadily declined during this century. Reasons include public reaction against authority of all kinds, increased educational level in the congregation, media exposure of unauthentic leaders, secularization, and inept shepherding. The admiration that people pour out upon those who produce impressive materialistic results is paltry compared to the esteem true Christians have for godly, gracious, and gifted leaders.

3

The Role of Leadership
Service

Guidelines for leadership behavior must develop out of a fundamental definition of leadership role as outlined in Scripture. Only then can the duties and functions of leaders be determined. What is the place of spiritual leadership in the church? The way leaders behave in a host of existential situations is governed by the position they see themselves occupying in the church.

The most crucial questions concerning church leadership include the following: Are church leaders placed among members or are church leaders placed over members? Are leaders to control the church and make decisions for the church, or is the church to participate in making major decisions? Should the church defer to its leaders' determination of the will of God, or should leaders defer to group determination of God's will? Answers to these questions determine how leaders actually conduct themselves in their ministries.

Some texts, for example, 1 Thessalonians 5:12 and Hebrews 13:17, seem to suggest that leaders of the church are to be authoritarian. Other texts stress service, not authority. These texts (e.g., Matt. 20:25–26; 1 Pet. 5:3) specifically prohibit leaders from exercising authority in the same manner as Gentile officials. Interpretation of these texts is crucial to determining leadership role.

Leaders who stress leadership authority and domination of church decision making generally see themselves as part of a hierarchal system, and their behavior patterns typically match that concept. Such people usually visualize themselves as between God and the church. They think God's will is mediated to the church through the leaders, much as God declared his will through Moses. In this understanding, leaders are in charge of those below them on the organizational chart. Subordinates take directions from those above them and give directions to those under them. Leaders (usually pastors) who conceptualize their roles as chief executive officers typically behave like heads, benevolent autocrats who give orders and expect deference from those under them (though they sometimes consult with subordinates). This understanding of leadership position is fundamental to a bureaucratic perception of church structure not unlike that of many secular organizations.

Other church leaders see themselves as servants or as participating members of a team and, as a result, their behavior radically differs from that of autocrats. Team leaders see others as colleagues, not as subordinates. Participatory leaders view decision making as shared responsibility, especially as issues become increasingly important. These leaders expect to defer to the group rather than expect the group to defer to them. Many routine matters are unilaterally decided by such leaders, but the authority and responsibility for making those decisions have been delegated by the group, usually in accordance with the church by-laws or policy manual.

Various leaders in the church have differing specific roles depending upon the office or position held. Pastors/elders have role definitions congruent to that office; deacons have somewhat different role definitions; the chairwoman of the Women's Missionary Society has a special role; and so forth. Role definitions, however, should not be made on the basis of professional versus nonprofessional status. Role distinctions must be made on the basis of call, differing gifts, and specialized training. God gifts, calls, and equips leaders for different positions of responsibility in the church. In spite of the considerable differences in specialized role definitions,

Scripture seems clear that all leaders are to be characterized by an attitude and a modus operandi of servanthood.

Ambiguity, Confusion, and Conflict

There is great ambiguity, confusion, and conflict in understanding church leadership roles and the relationships among these positions. It is not unusual to find leaders in the church (including pastors) who simply do not know what they are supposed to be or do.

Beginning with the research of H. Richard Niebuhr and Samuel Blizzard in the 1950s, pastoral role ambiguity, confusion, and conflict have been examined thoroughly.[1] Unfortunately, although the pastoral role has been studied and restudied, little has been written about the relationships between professional clergy and lay leaders, particularly in the understanding of authority and the decision-making process. Despite many surveys and studies, the subject of leadership role is perplexing.

Many church leaders are fuzzy about their mission, their place, and their responsibilities. Consequently, they typically do what necessity and urgency seem to demand, what they feel most pressured to do at the moment. They lack focus, direction, and clarity about their task and function. Leaders scurry to plug gaps, pump up programs, meet a variety of apparent needs, and produce statistical results—all without a clear concept, a theoretical model of what they are and what they should be doing.

Leaders have done much to corrupt their own positions and role definitions in the church. Failure to conceptualize all church leadership roles in terms of ministry has caused havoc in churches and a lack of orientation to spiritual mission, as Robert A. Raines has emphasized: "How tragically we succumb to the secular pressures upon us. How rapidly we lose our zeal, our sense of urgency. How easily we accept the pattern imposed upon us by our culture. . . . We prostitute our mission to the world. . . . We externalize our mission so that it becomes wrapped up in statistics and structure."[2]

1. For summaries of research on the pastoral role, see John Harris, *Stress, Power, and Ministry* (Washington, D.C.: Alban Institute, 1979), and Donald Smith, *Clergy in the Cross-Fire* (Philadelphia: Westminster, 1978).
2. Robert A. Raines, *New Life in the Church* (New York: Harper and Row, 1961), 15.

The stress spiritual leaders feel is frequently, if not chiefly, caused by the internal and external pressures of ambiguity and confusion. "[T]hese varied role pressures pile, one upon the other, in rapid fire. . . . [An] apt analogy may be that of machine guns, grenades, and booby traps going off . . . all at once."[3] Church strife, interpersonal conflict, spiritual impotency, and many other neurotic symptoms in today's churches are often the results of these role pressures and the failure to meet them successfully.

Frame of Reference

Despite the significant differences in individual roles, leaders need a frame of reference that encompasses all spiritual leadership. What is an adequate integrative concept of a leadership role, regardless of the particular position held? What is a church leader? What forms the foundation upon which all leadership roles are defined in the church and from which all leadership behavior must flow? Answers to these questions should be founded on the following scriptural teaching.

The heart of spiritual leadership is service, not headship. Leaders are not headmasters or controllers, but ministers. Leaders must be "eager to serve; not lording it over [followers]" (1 Pet. 5:3). Three Greek words are translated "minister" in the New Testament.[4] Paul used all of them in reference to himself as a servant of Christ. Spiritual leaders must understand that their role is service, not autocratic control. Christ must be recognized as in control. To serve Christ, the head, is to serve his church. Hence, biblical leadership is always servant-leadership. Leadership is under the headship of Christ and exists for the express purpose of serving the church, equipping the saints, and enabling their ministry to the world.

Christ's teaching (after washing the disciples' feet) is indisput-

3. Smith, *Clergy in the Cross-Fire*, 27.

4. *Diakonos:* a servant, attendant, minister, deacon (Mark 10:43; Rom. 13:4; 15:8; 1 Cor. 3:5; 2 Cor. 3:6; 6:4; 11:15; Gal. 2:17; Eph. 6:21; Col. 1:7, 23, 25; 4:7; 1 Thess. 3:2; 1 Tim. 4:6; *leitourgos:* one who served in a public office at his own expense; a public servant, minister. In the New Testament the word is used of Christ (Heb. 8:2), of angels (Heb. 1:7), of Paul (Rom. 15:16), of Epaphroditus (Phil. 2:15), and of secular rulers (Rom. 13:6); *hupēretēs:* literally, an underrower (*huper*, under; *ērētes*, a rower); hence, any subordinate acting under another's direction (Luke 4:20; Acts 26:16; 1 Cor. 4:1).

ably clear: "I have set you an example that you should do as I have done for you" (John 13:15). The disciples, who were to become leaders in his church, were never to think of themselves as above menial service. If any thought of themselves as important enough to be served by others, they were thereby disqualified for leadership. Paul taught, "Your attitude should be the same as that of Christ Jesus: Who, being in very nature God, did not consider equality with God something to be grasped, but made himself nothing, taking the very nature of a servant" (Phil. 2:5–7).

Every church leader should note that this biblical concept of leadership is directly opposed to the leadership philosophy prevalent in secular society. In the view of the world, leaders are served by followers; the more who serve the leader, the greater the leader. Jesus specifically rejected this Gentile understanding of leadership: "Not so with you. Instead, whoever wants to become great among you must be your servant, and whoever wants to be first must be your slave" (Matt. 20:28). Christ offered himself as the model for this concept of leadership; he "did not come to be served, but to serve" (Matt. 20:28).

Church leaders are always ministers regardless of individual position. The word *minister* carries with it the description of the role:

> We [must] remember that the word "ministry" serves not only to designate the full number of the church's leaders, but also to designate the true meaning of Christian leadership, the essential character which qualifies and unites all true leaders of the church—unites them with one another and with Christ, "who came not to be ministered unto, but to minister, and give his life a ransom for many" (Mark 10:45).[5]

Spiritual leaders were never intended to be authority figures to followers, but fellow workers, servants, and colleagues in the work of the ministry. Leaders in the church exist to facilitate the ministry of the whole body; they are not appointed to dominate or control the body.

This is not to say, however, that church leaders have no authority or power. Leaders certainly do have authority, but authority of a different kind, an authority that is uniquely Christian.

5. H. Richard Niebuhr, *The Purpose of the Church and Its Ministry* (New York: Harper and Brothers, 1956), 2.

Enormous conflict is caused in the church when leaders fail to recognize the centrality of the servant orientation and, consequently, fail to respond appropriately to that orientation. Leaders who behave like lords or dictators frequently become obnoxious to their followers. Dissension, resistance, and sometimes rebellion result when leaders dominate followers. Sometimes, of course, authoritarian leaders succeed in silencing or forcing out of the church all dissenters, leaving themselves firmly in control of the submissive people who are left. Such leaders generally succeed in presiding over weak, acquiescing people, not over mature, thinking, contributing Christians.

Servant-leadership does not mean that sometimes one leads and at other times one serves. Rather, it means that the leader best leads by serving; more than this, it means that one leads only by serving. Leadership is tested and authenticated by the measure of service rendered, not by effecting followers' compliance.

How then are we to interpret and understand 1 Thessalonians 5:12, Hebrews 13:17, and similar texts? The authority referred to in these verses is not the authority of leaders to inflict their will upon congregations, but their authority to proclaim the Word of God. The sense in which leaders are "over" followers is in their proclamation of scriptural truth. The obedience required of followers is an obedience to the Word when it is accurately and faithfully proclaimed by preacher-teachers. The author of Hebrews wrote: "Remember your leaders, who spoke the word of God to you. Consider the outcome of their way of life and imitate their faith" (13:7). Followers are commanded to "imitate their faith," not defer to their will in personal or corporate matters. "Rule" is authoritative declaration and application of God's Word (not personal opinion) to the activities of individuals and the church.[6] Those leaders who deceptively mix God's authoritative Word with their personal viewpoints do the church a disservice. Some leaders apparently are unable to distinguish their ideas from God's will and, therefore, present their goals as the plan of God.

Building upon the basic concept of servant-leadership, Scripture outlines how this role is to be fulfilled in the church.

6. This interpretation is the position of John R. W. Stott, Jay Adams, and many others. It is more fully discussed later in this book.

Spiritual Leaders Are Examples

Role clarification for all spiritual servant-leadership begins with the basic understanding that leaders are models for the church. The New Testament repeatedly advises leaders to "set an example for the believers in speech, in life, in love, in faith and in purity" (1 Tim. 4:12). Paul was so conscious of his responsibility in this area that he "worked night and day, laboring and toiling so that [he] would not be a burden to any. . . . [He] did this, not because [he did] not have the right to such [monetary] help, but in order to make [himself] a model for you to follow" (2 Thess. 3:8–9).

The most fundamental leadership need of the church is visible demonstration of spiritual discipleship. Leaders must be able to say, "This is what it means to be a disciple of Jesus Christ." Paul counseled Titus, "In everything set them an example by doing what is good. In your teaching show integrity, seriousness and soundness of speech that cannot be condemned, so that those who oppose you may be ashamed because they have nothing bad to say about us" (Titus 2:7–8).

Spiritual leadership begins with setting an example of "righteousness, godliness, faith, love, endurance and gentleness" (1 Tim. 6:11). The deepest truths cannot always be verbalized, but leaders must be able to say: "Follow my example, as I follow the example of Christ" (1 Cor. 11:1) and "You yourselves know how you ought to follow our example" (2 Thess. 3:7).

The test of effective spiritual leadership is whether the leader can say to followers: "You know how we lived among you for your sake. You became imitators of us and of the Lord" (1 Thess. 1:5–6). Failing in this, leadership has failed in its most crucial activity.

Charles Spurgeon told of the man who preached so well but lived so badly that when he was in the pulpit everybody said he ought never to come out again, and when he was out of it, they all declared he ought never to enter it again. No gifts or abilities can make up for a lifestyle that belies one's profession. John taught, "Whoever claims to live in him must walk as Jesus did" (1 John 2:6). This is certainly and especially true for leaders.

Role definition in the church begins in being, not doing. Character and role are blended inseparably in ministry. The first duty of the leader, regardless of position, gifts, or calling, is to model scriptural truth. Leaders "are entrusted with God's work" (Titus

1:7) in a way in which others are not. For that reason every spiritual leader must be exemplary in behavior and lifestyle. No spiritual leadership can take place without it.

Spiritual Leaders Are Stewards

Spiritual leaders are stewards; they are people entrusted with caretaker or trustee responsibilities. The responsibility, particularly for elders, is that of spiritual oversight of the church.

The word *overseer* (Greek *episkopos*, bishop) is used seven times in the New Testament, six times in reference to human leadership of the church and once in reference to Christ (1 Pet. 2:25). The overseer is "entrusted with God's work" (Titus 1:7) and this is "a noble task" (1 Tim. 3:1) conferred upon spiritual leaders by the Holy Spirit (Acts 20:28).

While the word *overseer* refers particularly to the distinct responsibilities of the bishop, elder, or pastor, the broader truth is that all spiritual leadership entails stewardship. God's servant is charged to "guard the good deposit that was entrusted to you—guard it with the help of the Holy Spirit who lives in us" (2 Tim. 1:14). Paul linked the concept of servanthood with that of stewardship: "So then, men ought to regard us as servants of Christ and as those entrusted with the secret things of God. Now it is required that those who have been given a trust must prove faithful" (1 Cor. 4:1–2).

The essential idea of this sacred trust is not that of administration, although the word *overseer* has frequently been misused by church leaders to justify excessive administrative work. Rather, the idea is that the spiritual leaders are to "keep watch over [the church] as men who must give an account" (Heb. 13:17) and thereby "to present to you the word of God in its fullness" (Col. 1:25) with the object of "admonishing and teaching everyone with all wisdom, so that we may present everyone perfect in Christ" (Col. 1:28).

The words *overseer* and *steward* as used in the New Testament never imply autocratic control. Instead, the picture is that of "a mother caring for her little children" (1 Thess. 2:7) or that of a father "encouraging, comforting, and urging you to live lives worthy of God" (1 Thess. 2:12). Guardianship and tutelage, rather than administration and management, are indicated in the fundamental meaning of stewardship. Leaders who become bogged down in clerical chores, often to serve materialistic ends, simply fail to provide true spiritual leadership. The oversight required is not of organizational hierarchy and jurisdictional control, but of spiritual supervision.

Most spiritual leaders, especially pastors, of course have some administrative responsibilities. Leaders must not use the concept of stewardship as an excuse for shoddy administration. Leaders should have administrative skills and perform administrative tasks efficiently, leaving time for biblical stewardship, that is, spiritual oversight. Fundamental to the role of servant-leader is spiritual oversight, not organizational management. Leaders who spend 50 to 70 percent of their work time in administration cannot possibly fulfill their role as spiritual overseers.

Church Leaders Are Shepherds

The metaphorical emphasis upon spiritual leaders as shepherds is ingrained in Scripture and is closely associated with spiritual oversight. The concept of the spiritual shepherd was first used in the New Testament by Jesus: "I am the good shepherd. The good shepherd lays down his life for the sheep" (John 10:11). The same word (Greek *poimēn*) was used by Paul in Ephesians 4:11 and is frequently translated "pastor." Peter exhorted the elders: "Be shepherds of God's flock that is under your care" (1 Pet. 5:2). Paul charged the elders of Ephesus to "be shepherds of the church of God" (Acts 20:28).

Of course, the shepherding role is usually considered to be a function of the professional staff, the clergy. This is unfortunate, because the shepherding role applies to all church leaders who are involved in ministry. Shepherding is not the exclusive prerogative of clergy, but of all spiritual leaders. All spiritual leaders, especially those who preach and teach, are undershepherds.

Several important truths are inherent in the shepherding role of church leaders.

First, shepherds must genuinely care for the people under their oversight. The following passage is a severe denunciation of leaders who care for themselves rather than for the people: "[B]ecause my shepherds did not search for my flock but cared for themselves rather than for my flock, therefore, O shepherds, hear the word of the LORD: . . . I am against the shepherds and will hold them accountable for my flock. I will remove them from tending the flock. . . ." (Ezek. 34:8–10). Jesus contrasted his ministry with that of one who "runs away because he is a hired hand and cares nothing for the sheep" (John 10:13). The uncaring shepherd is an anomaly.

Many people in today's churches feel used rather than cared for by their leaders. People resent being pawns on the leader's chessboard or building blocks for the leader's personal kingdom. Genuine care for the spiritual and physical welfare of the church as a whole and for members in particular is indispensable to spiritual leadership.

Many leaders really do care, but they are unable to demonstrate their care in meaningful ways. Such leaders are often falsely viewed as personal glory seekers or manipulators.

Second, the shepherding role carries the responsibility of nurture. Leaders must provide spiritual food and protection for the church body. Timothy was exhorted, "Devote yourself to the public reading of Scripture, to preaching and to teaching" (1 Tim. 4:13). Overseers must be "able to teach" (1 Tim. 3:2).

The earliest church leaders observed, "It would not be right for us to neglect the ministry of the word of God in order to wait on tables" (Acts 6:2). Therefore, others were selected for these administrative functions so that pastoral leaders could nurture the people through preaching and teaching. This lesson is frequently forgotten in the modern passion for secularization which has bogged down spiritual leaders with many trivial or materialistic concerns. Spiritual leaders must nurture, edify, disciple, and equip the saints for their ministry in the world.

Third, the indispensable correlate to good preaching and teaching is study. The chief (but not the only) evidence of a fragmented and secularized church is dryness in the pulpit and the classroom and boredom among church members.[7] Every effective church—not, however, every large church—has been built upon solid preaching and teaching by its spiritual leaders who have been students of the Word of God. Sizable churches can be built without solid biblical exposition, but spiritually potent and ministerially effective churches cannot.

Fourth, the shepherding role demands guidance. Christ's scath-

7. Every leader who preaches or teaches should read William A. Quayle, "The Sin of Being Uninteresting," in *The Pastor-Preacher* (Grand Rapids: Baker, 1979), 140, and Charles Spurgeon, "Attention!" in *Lectures to My Students* (reprint ed.; Grand Rapids: Zondervan, 1954), 127.

ing words to the religious leaders were: "You blind guides!" (Matt. 23:24). True spiritual leadership necessitates guidance like that of an excellent father in his home, for "if anyone does not know how to manage [Greek *proïstēmi*, attend to] his own family, how can he take care of [Greek *epimeleomai*, to take care of, involving forethought and provision] God's church?" (1 Tim. 3:5).[8] The father's excellence in family leadership does not mean high-handed control, but inspirational guidance and protection.[9]

Guidance means enlightenment, tutoring, motivation, and persuasion. Guidance is supervised assistance. Enabled by their experience, training, and wisdom, guides accompany, direct, advise, and counsel. Some may be gifted and trained to provide this guidance in spiritual matters, and others may be equipped to guide in temporal concerns. Leaders are guides for their followers, and this truth applies to all of the church's leaders.

Many church leaders stop functioning as spiritual leaders and allow their roles to become externalized and stripped of the central, biblical role definitions. Every church leader, particularly pastors, ought to reflect soberly upon the following scathing words:

> The fact is . . . that too many [leaders] are more enthusiastic about the activities of the church, the operation of its machinery, the size of its membership, the amount of its budgets, the cultural life and social problems of society, the passage of laws by legislative bodies, the promotion of human improvement programs—all of which are good and necessary—than about the gospel and the transforming power of God. To deal with the visible and the tangible is much easier and, for the time being, more interesting, perhaps, more rewarding, than to deal with the invisible and the intangible.[10]

Such leaders have forsaken their true calling. Many churches eventually become disillusioned with such leaders.

Spiritual servant-leaders must realize that the central tasks that

8. The Greek word *epimeleomai* is used in the New Testament only in this verse and in Luke 10:34–35, where it refers to the good Samaritan's care for an injured man, a significant association.

9. See John R. W. Stott, *The Preacher's Portrait* (Grand Rapids: Eerdmans, 1961), for a discussion of spiritual leaders as spiritual fathers and guides. Spurgeon also discusses this matter in his *All-Round Ministry* (reprint ed.; Carlisle, Penn.: Banner of Truth, 1972).

10. Ilion Jones, *The Pastor: The Man and His Ministry* (Philadelphia: Westminster, 1961), 63.

define their roles have to do with study, prayer, modeling, discipling, preaching, teaching, and equipping saints for ministry. All
must be done with the attitude of humble service to Christ and
his church. This is leadership, not by secular criteria, but by the
standards of the body of Christ and Scripture.

Church leaders who settle for jobs that promote, maintain, and
manage a religious institution and a plethora of programs are pa-
thetic caricatures of spiritual leaders. Churches, on the other hand,
must insist that their leaders major in the functions of ministry,
not in tasks associated with organizational machinery. Many
churches are organized in a way that prohibits their leaders from
fulfilling biblical leadership roles. Spiritual leaders frequently want
desperately to function as God intended, but are frustrated by pressures to "run the church" and make the church "successful" by
materialistic standards.

Spiritual leaders must patiently teach the church a proper understanding of leadership's role, and the church must allow itself to
be taught. Churches that do not allow their leaders to function as
God intends seriously hurt themselves, whether or not the church
prospers by materialistic standards.

None of this excuses carelessness in administrative tasks, however, and we must recognize that administration itself is a form of
ministry. Some leaders are gifted and called to administer. But
management of programs and administrative efficiency are not the
heart of ministerial servant-leadership in the church. Spiritual
leaders who achieve excellence in the central tasks of their ministry
will do much to alleviate the tension, conflict, and spiritual impotency of the typical church. Elders and deacons especially must
be concerned with fulfilling functions, primarily spiritual direction, congruent to their office.

Summary

Leadership behavior stems from role definition. There is much
ambiguity, confusion, and conflict in the understanding of the distinct roles of spiritual leaders. This has caused spiritual impotence,
disunity, and dysfunction in the church.

Central to the role definition of any spiritual leader, regardless
of specific task, is the concept of service to Christ and to the
church. Servant-leaders are examples to the church, stewards for

the church, and shepherds in the church. Inherent in such an understanding of spiritual leadership is the responsibility to study the Word of God in order to effectively nurture, feed, and guide the congregation.

Spiritual leaders who settle for a secularized role definition (i.e., administration of organizational machinery) have forsaken their true calling and have prostituted their mission in the church and the world. A return to an emphasis upon and excellency in these central, scriptural responsibilities is overdue. The primary duties of spiritual leaders involve modeling, praying, preaching, teaching, discipling, and equipping the members for their ministries in the world.

4

The Task of Leadership
Enablement

O nce the fundamental concept of leadership role is defined, leaders can begin to clarify their task. *Role* primarily has to do with being, while *task* focuses on doing. What does the church leader need to accomplish? What is the fundamental responsibility of a leader? What must spiritual leaders do to fulfill their mission?

At this point, a clear understanding of the meaning of leadership, particularly spiritual leadership, is necessary. How is leadership, suitable for a church setting, defined?

A Definition of Leadership

Leadership is characterized and described in a variety of ways by different authors, each writing from within a certain organizational framework. There are literally hundreds of different definitions of leadership. A sampling may be helpful:

Interpersonal influence exercised in a situation and directed, through the communication process, toward the attainment of a special goal or goals.[1]

A learned behavioral skill which includes the ability to help others achieve their potential as individuals and team members.[2]

Leadership . . . is the process of persuasion and example by which an individual (or leadership team) induces a group to take action that is in accord with the leader's purposes or the shared purposes of all.[3]

Each definition contains some insight, yet each seems to fall short in some respect, especially when we consider spiritual leadership in the church.

Our definition seems to fit spiritual leadership best:

Spiritual leadership is the development of relationships with the people of a Christian institution or body in such a way that individuals and the group are enabled to formulate and achieve biblically compatible goals that meet real needs. By their ethical influence, spiritual leaders serve to motivate and enable others to achieve what otherwise would never be achieved.

One crucial ingredient in this definition is the emphasis upon others' (group and individual) goals, not the personal goals of the leader. In other words, spiritual leaders do not unilaterally decide what others should do and then try to get followers to do it. Or, to put the same thought in conventional Christian language, leaders do not determine the will of God for the group or church and then attempt to persuade others to follow it. Rather, leaders stimulate and aid the members to identify and achieve their own goals.

Of course, certain goals are biblically defined and, when those goals are clear, the spiritual leader's responsibility is to enable constituents to grasp and understand them, adopt them, and then achieve them. In other words, group process is not necessary to determine that loving one another should be a goal. Such a goal is

1. Paul Hersey and Kenneth Blanchard, *Management of Organizational Behavior* (Englewood Cliffs, N.J.: Prentice-Hall, 1982), 84.

2. Jerry Robinson and Roy Clifford, *Leadership Roles in Community Groups* (Urbana-Champaign, Ill.: University of Illinois, 1975), 2.

3. John W. Gardner, *The Nature of Leadership: Introductory Considerations* (Washington, D.C.: Independent Sector, 1986), 6.

biblically mandated. Leaders need only to point out the scriptural admonition to love and present it to the church with authority. However, leaders must recognize the fundamental difference between biblical goals and their personal opinions about church decisions.

Another important factor in the preceding definition is the emphasis upon service to the group, not control over the group. Manipulation or coercion of people to achieve what the leader wants is not true leadership. John W. Gardner is correct:

> Elements of physical coercion are involved in some kinds of leadership and of course there is psychological coercion, however mild and subtle, including peer pressure, in all social action. But in our culture popular understanding of the term [leadership] distinguishes it from coercion—and places higher on the scale of leadership those forms involving lesser degrees of coercion.[4]

In this regard, Ted W. Engstrom's statement is disconcerting: "Acting in our managerial capacity, all of us [leaders] . . . do basically the same thing. We are each and all engaged in part in getting things done with and through people."[5] This statement implies that the leader uses or manages people to get things done, and that the things done are what the leader decides should be done. Such a philosophy is consistent with many modern business and political concepts of leadership, but is incompatible with the kind of spiritual leadership that scrupulously avoids manipulation. People are not to be used to further the plans of leaders. People must be respected, involved in the setting of their own goals, and treated like colleagues in the ministry.

An enabling philosophy of church leadership always stresses profound respect for people. In the best forms of leadership, people are not treated as subjects or herded like cattle. Some of the most successful business enterprises claim this philosophy of respect:

> IBM's philosophy is largely contained in three simple beliefs. I want to begin with what I think is the most important: *our respect for the individual*. This is a simple concept, but in IBM it occupies a major portion of management time. . . . Treating people—not money,

4. Ibid.
5. Ted W. Engstrom, *The Making of a Christian Leader* (Grand Rapids: Zondervan, 1976), 137.

machines, or minds—as the natural resource may be the key to it
all. . . . Treat people as adults; treat them as partners; treat them
with dignity; treat them with respect.[6]

Leadership that is compatible with scriptural guidelines can
only be other-centered; it can never be leader-centered. This is the
transforming leadership articulated and advocated by James Burns:
"Such leadership occurs when one or more persons *engage* with
others in such a way that leaders and followers raise one another
to higher levels of motivation and morality."[7] By these criteria,
those who exercise authoritarian control to achieve their own
objectives are not really leaders. They are power wielders who
"constantly exploit their external resources (economic, social,
psychological, and institutional) and their 'effectance,' their training, skill, and competence, to make persons and things do what
they want done. The key factor here is indeed 'what they want
done.' "[8]

The classical power philosophies of Machiavelli, Hobbes, and
Nietzsche may guide the behavior of the world's dictators, but they
are grossly inconsistent with true, ethical leadership and the Word
of God. If we judge according to a high standard of leadership,
Hitler, Idi Amin, and Jim Jones (and not a few contemporary church
figures) were never leaders despite enormous but temporary power
and materialistic success. Louis B. Lundborg succinctly states this
truth: "A leader is one whom others will follow willingly and vol-
untarily. That rules out tyrants, bullies, autocrats, and all others
who use coercive power to impose their wills on others."[9] Or as
Kenneth O. Gangel correctly observes: "Leadership is not political
power-play . . . leadership is not authoritarian attitude . . . leadership is not cultic control."[10]

Yet, we must never think that a leader is powerless. Indeed, to
suggest that a leader is without authority is to pose the anomaly
of a leader with no followers. Leadership is a special kind of authority: legitimized power—the power of ethical, inspiring influ-

6. Thomas Peters and Robert Waterman, *In Search of Excellence* (New York: Warner,
1982), 14, 39, 238.
7. James Burns, *Leadership* (New York: Harper and Row, 1979), 20.
8. Ibid., 14.
9. Louis B. Lundborg, *The Art of Being an Executive* (New York: Free Press, 1981),
85.
10. Kenneth O. Gangel, *Competent to Lead* (Chicago: Moody, 1974), 11–13.

ence and enablement. This kind of authority can be awesome in its effect upon individuals and groups. It is the kind of power an excellent teacher or guide brings to bear upon the people he or she serves. It scrupulously avoids manipulative tactics to enhance the leader's status or to accomplish the leader's agenda.

The real and ultimate test of genuine leadership is the realization of enduring change that meets people's most basic physical, emotional, and spiritual needs. The world's and the church's appraisal of leadership frequently is false. There is the almost irresistible tendency to judge leadership by production statistics and materialistic standards, and to grant esteem and promotion to such "successful" people. But if actual needs in the lives of others are not met, and if people are not evangelized and edified, no meaningful spiritual leadership has taken place despite whatever achievement might be considered successful or significant.

Leadership and Management

We should distinguish between leadership and management, although sometimes the differences are pushed too far and become contrived. There is overlap between leadership and management and the dissimilarities are not always sharply defined. A good leader must have some good management skills, and good managers usually have some leadership qualities. It is difficult to imagine a good manager who is not also a leader and vice versa. Nevertheless, there are some significant differences.

Vision

A leader has greater vision than a manager. Leaders think long-term, beyond the day-to-day operations, beyond the immediate horizons which often limit the vision of managers and followers. Leaders see the whole, including relationships between the parts and relationships between the immediate organization and other organizations.

Leaders envision the achievement of objectives never dreamed of by others. George Bernard Shaw said: "You see things; and you say, 'Why?' But I dream of things that never were; and I say, 'Why not?' " Leaders not only have such dreams but also inspire others to share those dreams.

Renewal

Leaders are always interested in revisions of process and structure, with an eye toward changing outmoded methods, defining new goals, tapping new resources, motivating or enlisting personnel, and invigorating the group and its individuals. Managers emphasize the achievement of goals already defined and the efficient use of present structures and readily available resources.

Managers give directions and evaluate performance, but leaders stimulate greater achievement and energize the entire organization—the group and its individuals. Leaders are more creative, innovative, and transforming than managers.

Leaders such as Gandhi can generate and inflame a worldwide movement. England desperately needed a leader capable of rallying the nation to fight against Hitler's forces, and Winston Churchill rose to become one of her greatest statesmen. From the Christian's standpoint, Jesus Christ was the greatest leader the world has seen. With a handful of rough-hewn disciples he founded a kingdom that shall never end, one against which the gates of hell shall not prevail. By the power of his person, his example, his teaching, and his Spirit, he changed the world forever.

Orientation

Leaders are people-oriented; they constantly think in terms of their constituents and their needs. Managers tend to be more product- and program-oriented. Managers think about getting jobs done, doing things to produce satisfactory results according to set criteria. Leaders think about doing right things to help people maximize their potential.

Managers are conscious of efficiency, but leaders are conscious of values. Managers are quick to direct people; leaders are quick to listen to people. A manager might say, "It can't be done," or "Maybe we can do it if . . ."; a leader would say, "We must find a way to do it, and we will." Managers supervise people, but leaders energize people.

Leadership Strategies

What do leaders do in the exercise of spiritual enablement? By what ethical and biblically compatible methodologies do they operate so that leaders and followers raise one another to higher levels of spiritual achievement and realization? What special responsibilities do leaders accept in carrying out their unique influence in the church? There are five fundamental activities in the leader's task of spiritual enablement.

Leaders Listen

Leaders must have a passionate desire to understand the hurts, longings, desires, temptations, sins, joys, and real needs of groups and individuals that form their constituency.

Leadership involves effective communication, and effective communication begins with listening.

> True listening builds strength in other people. . . . The best test of whether we are communicating at this depth is to ask ourselves first: Are we really listening? Are we listening to the one we want to communicate to? Is our basic attitude, as we approach the confrontation, one of wanting to understand? Remember that great line from the prayer of St. Francis, "Lord, grant that I may not seek so much to be understood as to understand."[11]

Every real spiritual leader echoes this prayer of Saint Francis.

Church leaders must develop this aptitude for listening. The counsel of James should never be forgotten: "My dear brothers, take note of this: Everyone should be quick to listen, slow to speak" (1:19). This wisdom is as old as Solomon: "Let the wise listen and add to their learning, and let the discerning get guidance. . . . Listen to advice and accept instruction, and in the end you will be wise" (Prov. 1:5; 19:20).

In the context of leadership, the word *listen* is used in its widest possible connotation. Leaders give close attention to their constituents; they have their fingers on the pulse of the group. Leaders know the heartbeat of individual people; they know what gripes them and what fulfills their dreams. They know the real, but often unspoken, needs and hopes.

No one can be a wise leader who fails to listen, learn, and accept the counsel of mature people. Untold suffering has been inflicted upon the church and its members by those in official positions who have been so passionate about carrying out a private agenda

11. Robert Greenleaf, *Servant Leadership* (New York: Paulist, 1977), 17.

that they fail to listen to the heartthrobs of the community—the congregation and its individuals.

True leadership begins with the act of hearing. Leadership action that is not based on careful listening is apt to be the wrong action. Listening with the ears and the heart must become so fundamental a part of every leader's life that the first and most natural thing the leader does is listen attentively. Obviously, the leader must listen to God, but also to God's people.

Leaders Build a Team

Effective leaders never bring others to submission, but bring them to active participation in the life, maturing, decision making, and outreach of the church. Saints are made by gaining their partnership, not their obeisance. Therefore, there is no alternative to the promotion of a sense of collegiality, a team spirit in ministry. The leader uses his influence to build a team. Moses thought he could do everything alone, but Jethro told him in essence: "You can't do it alone; you need a team to share the responsibilities!" A wise leader heeds Jethro's advice.

Effective churches are led by those who build a strong sense of synergism, community, and solidarity between leaders and constituents (the word *follower* seems too passive). With this approach to leadership the distinction between leaders and those led often blurs in the emphasis upon collegiality and fraternity. Just who is leading and who is following may not be readily apparent, but this is not important.

Paul obviously made team building a major emphasis in his ministry. He commonly spoke of people as his brothers or sisters, his fellow workers, and his fellow soldiers. Paul took pains to correct a wrong attitude in the church at Corinth: "For when one says, 'I follow Paul,' and another, 'I follow Apollos,' are you not mere men? What, after all, is Apollos? And what is Paul? Only servants, through whom you came to believe—as the Lord has assigned to each his task . . . for we are God's fellow workers" (1 Cor. 3:4–5, 9). Paul's goal was never to get people to do what he personally wanted them to do, but to do what was clearly the desire of God. Paul dissuaded people from following him except insofar as he followed Christ. Paul expressed great joy "because of your partnership in the gospel from the first day until now" (Phil. 1:5). The best churches have members who do not feel like spectators or subjects, but like participants and fellow workers with their leaders.

Robert Greenleaf puts this concept simply, bluntly, and beautifully: "And if one is to preside over a successful business, one's major talent will need to evolve from being the *chief* into the *builder of the team.*"[12] The Japanese have excelled in this concept of leadership in corporate enterprise, and it has rewarded them richly. If Greenleaf's concept is valid and effective in the business world, it is vastly more important in the church. This is New Testament leadership at its best.

Leaders Inspire

As Burns suggests, "The first task of leadership is to bring to consciousness the followers' sense of their own needs, values, and purposes."[13] Spiritual leaders inspire people to recognize their own spiritual needs, values, and objectives, and then facilitate growth in these vital areas. Good, effective spiritual leaders infuse others with an animating, quickening, and exalting spirit of enthusiasm for the person of Christ, growth in Christ, and the mission of the church.

To inspire is a task of a good teacher, and a leader is always a teacher of sorts:

Teachers . . . treat students neither coercively nor instrumentally but as joint seekers of truth and of mutual actualization. They help students define moral values not by imposing their own moralities on them but by positing situations that pose hard moral choices and then encouraging conflict and debate. They seek to help students rise to higher stages of moral reasoning and hence to higher levels of principled judgment. Throughout, teachers provide a social and intellectual environment in which students can *learn.*[14]

If a spiritual leader truly wants others to learn, and if he is to inspire them, he needs to demonstrate worthwhile truths in his own life. "The fact is . . . nothing leads as well as example. . . . [V]alues and behavioral norms are simply not transmitted easily by talk or memo, but are conveyed very effectively by doing and

12. Ibid., 72.
13. Burns, *Leadership*, 41.
14. David McClelland, *Power: The Inner Experience* (New York: Irvington, 1975), 260.

doing *visibly.*"[15] In Paul's words, "Follow my example, as I follow the example of Christ" (1 Cor. 11:1).

Leaders Focus on Values

Good spiritual leaders do not focus on machinery, programs, or statistics. They are passionate about the fundamentals of value systems, reasons, philosophies, intrinsic truths, structures, objectives, designs, moods, emotions, and environments. All of this may be thought of as an essential part of a philosophy of ministry, and every excellent leader has an uncommonly clear understanding of these things.

For example, poor leaders might give great attention to the details of running a vacation Bible school, down to the cookies and punch, but they may have little idea of why all of this is being done and what is to be achieved by doing all these conventional things. Such people might be good workers and detail persons (managers of sorts), but they are not leaders because they do not focus on causes, values, or objectives. They see the cookies, punch, crayons, and chalkboards, but they do not see exactly how this program can meet fundamental needs and integrate into other activities of the church.

The trouble with many churches is that their leaders are doing many unnecessary things (and doing them well, perhaps), and they don't know why they are doing them, except that they are expected and customary. In the meantime, many things that desperately need to be done are overlooked because of this maintenance mentality and devotion to tradition.

The real leader is always aware of a set of underlying values, perhaps not verbalized publicly, that is capable of impelling the institution or group forward. As Philip Selznick stated, "The institutional leader, then, is primarily an expert in the promotion and protection of values."[16] Or as Thomas Peters and Robert Waterman observed, "We are struck by the explicit attention [successful businesses] pay to values, and by the way in which their leaders have created exciting environments through personal attention, persistence, and direct intervention."[17]

15. Andrew Grove, *High Output Management* (New York: Random House, 1983), 52.
16. Philip Selznick, *Leadership and Administration* (Berkeley: University of California Press, 1984), 153.
17. Peters and Waterman, *In Search of Excellence*, 238.

It is because of this meticulous attention to value systems that good church leaders strive to maintain a climate where creative ideas, healthy conflict, and participation in decision making are welcomed. The task, in part, of the true leader is to make sure that innovative ideas are solicited and that the people with these ideas are encouraged to participate in the work of the ministry. All of this is influence, but of a kind that is ethically acceptable and necessary in the church.

Leaders Balance Priorities

There are three dimensions to effective church leadership: personal (the individual), social (the group), and production (the job). The good spiritual leader is able to keep all three focused at the same time, carefully balancing and assigning proper weight and attention to each, never sacrificing one in order to achieve the other.

They are poor leaders whose zeal to get the job done causes them to run roughshod over people, or whose passion for the group welfare makes them oblivious to the individual, or whose fervor to promote harmony leads them to achieve nothing but that. The best leaders excel in all three dimensions.

Jesus was zealous to accomplish his mission—the work the Father had given him to do—but he always had time to devote to individuals in need. He was eager to build the kingdom, but he never neglected the prostitute, the tax collector, or the blind man. He had time for the Samaritan woman and for Simon the Pharisee. He took time to feed the five thousand and to teach the disciples. Even in his agony on the cross, he was aware of and attentive to the needs of others ("Father, forgive them. . . ," "Woman, behold your son, . . ." and "Today you shall be with me . . ."). He was equally concerned for the individual, the larger group, and the task before him. Upon this three-cornered foundation he did all that he did. Indeed, these three seem to so blend in his ministry that they are inseparable and at times indistinguishable. He established his kingdom and accomplished the Father's will through giving attention to the individuals and the group of disciples.

Hence, the task of the true spiritual leader is to promote growth in competence, responsibility, character, and leadership in individuals, to produce a healthy, functioning, ministering body, and to promote the achievement of the church's goals and plans in its community. These three dimensions of ministry are always sharply focused and balanced in the minds and actions of good spiritual leaders.

By identifying the five major responsibilities of leaders we are not suggesting that these things form the leader's comprehensive action list. Far from it. In fulfilling the duties of leadership good leaders must, at various times, diagnose problems, gather and study facts, develop suggested solutions, evaluate alternatives, and make recommendations and decisions within specified guidelines. They may also plan, coordinate, publicize, introduce, clarify, restate, regulate, delegate, and summarize, much as a good manager might do. Yet, none of these things are done in a high-handed, dictatorial, or unilateral way, but in the spirit of humble service to God and to the church, and in collaboration and cooperation with other leaders and the whole group.

The good spiritual leader conceives every task in terms of service to Christ and his church. The leader doesn't work with a lofty, isolated spirit of superiority, but in the spirit of collegiality and unity with other servants in his church. Everything the leader does is done with the supreme consciousness that Christ is the head of the church and we are his servants here to accomplish his work. Real action comes through the inspiring influence and enablement of one who demonstrates the reality of living under the authority of the Word of God and the Spirit of God.

Summary

Spiritual leadership is the development of relationships with the people of a Christian organization, institution, or body in such a way that individuals and the group are enabled to formulate and achieve biblical goals that meet real needs. Leaders, by their ethical influence, serve to enable, motivate, and inspire others to achieve their goals.

There are some notable differences between leaders and managers. Leaders excel in vision, revitalizing and energizing structures, process, and constituents, and orientation to the real needs of people.

Real leaders must be distinguished from mere power wielders. Spiritual leaders never use people to accomplish their own agendas, but inspire others to achieve their own goals and, ultimately, biblical goals. The test of genuine leadership is change that meets group and individual needs and enables constituents to fulfill the will of God in their lives.

The primary tasks of good spiritual leaders in influencing the church are as follows:

1. Leaders listen. Their decisions and actions are based on real understanding of their constituency.
2. Leaders build collegiality. They never set out to use people to accomplish their goals and purposes. They disavow personal partisanship in favor of developing a team spirit and loyalty to Christ.
3. Leaders inspire. Good spiritual leaders infuse others with an animating, quickening, and exalting spirit of enthusiasm for the task of the church and the person of Christ. They do this primarily through their personal optimism, authenticity, enthusiasm, and example.
4. Leaders emphasize values. They focus on the fundamentals of value systems, reasons, philosophies, intrinsic truths, structures, objectives, designs, moods, emotions, and environments.
5. Leaders balance priorities. There is always consciousness of the individual, the group, and the job to be done. No one of these three is sacrificed for the benefit of the others.

In fulfilling these primary tasks of leadership, the spiritual leader may do a variety of other things, yet all is done under the headship of Christ and in the spirit of collegiality and service within the body.

Difficulties of Leadership in the Church

5

The Style of Leadership
Flexibility

Questions pertaining to leadership style often perplex leaders, especially those who sincerely desire to behave ethically and avoid manipulation. Leaders wonder, for instance, to what extent they should attempt to influence the decisions of the church, or what circumstances call for assertive or passive behavior.

One of the most obvious and oft-repeated truths about leadership is that there is no optimal style. No one can say that on a style scale of one to ten (with ten being the most aggressive) that a leader ought to be a six or an eight, for example. Andrew Grove expresses what everyone knows, almost by instinct, "The hard finding [of research] simply would not show that one style of leadership was better than another. It was hard to escape the conclusion that no optimal management style existed."[1]

In other words, research and common sense suggest that certain

---

1. Andrew Grove, *High Output Management* (New York: Random House, 1983), 175.

situations, environments, and constituents call for more aggressive behavior from leaders, and other circumstances demand less aggressive behavior from leaders. Some leaders are effective, on occasion, with considerable aggressiveness; others are equally effective with considerable submissiveness. Hence, flexibility in leadership style is a necessity.

The preceding chapters may suggest to the reader that spiritual leaders are prohibited from being aggressive (see, e.g., Matt. 20:25–26; 1 Pet. 5:3). This is not so. Leaders must not become dictators or mere power wielders; yet, there are times and situations when leaders must become quite aggressive in their ethical attempts to influence people and decisions. The best biblical leaders were sometimes very aggressive in leadership. It is crucial that spiritual leaders understand when such behavior is appropriate and compatible with scriptural guidelines.

The Continuum of Leadership Style

Many books about leadership contain various forms of a style continuum. Most look something like the one reproduced in figure 1. Others have three, five, or seven categories along the continuum and other labels (e.g., permissive, democratic, or benevolent dictator).

Some authors describe in painstaking detail the differences in the various classifications, almost as though the styles are absolute, clear-cut, easily recognized and differentiated. The truth is that one style fades imperceptibly into another style, and leadership behavior in real situations often combines styles. It is difficult, perhaps impossible, to decide exactly what style is being used on a given occasion except as the extremes on the continuum become obvious.

It is probably best to avoid an attempt to describe each of the various categories of style. Rather, it seems most profitable to note that some efforts to influence are more aggressive and others are

FIGURE 1
A Continuum of Leadership Styles

Laissez-faire	Participatory	Bureaucratic	Autocratic

less aggressive. Extremely aggressive behavior may be considered autocratic, and extremely submissive behavior may be considered laissez-faire, a virtual withdrawal of any attempt to influence. This may be pictured as in figure 2.

How are aggressiveness and submissiveness in leadership style characterized? It is somewhat risky to attempt to describe them because these labels can span such a wide range. Also, it is difficult to portray them without seeming to pass moral judgment. Nevertheless, an understanding of the attitudes and behaviors of these styles is crucial to leadership's decisions about the suitability of proposed actions.

Aggressive Leadership Behavior

Aggressive behavior is here described in its extreme form, which is called autocratic or authoritarian behavior. There are many lesser degrees of aggressiveness in which particular points may not be true, or are true to a lesser degree.

An extremely aggressive leadership action may indicate a lack of trust or confidence in other people. The aggressive church leader may feel it is necessary to take unilateral action or control the group process because he perceives others to be incompetent or insensitive to the will of God. Of course, there are times when group members may actually be incompetent, immature, or insensitive. Paul's first letter to the Corinthian church, for example, is extraordinarily directive, partly because of the immaturity of the church.

On the other hand, extremely aggressive leadership behavior may indicate a deep insecurity on the part of the leader. Autocrats find it difficult to yield to the opinions of others, often because their ideas are tied to their egos. They feel a need to be dominant and control people as a boost to their status or sense of power. When such leaders' ideas or opinions are rejected, they feel personally rebuffed, and hence, failures. Autocrats frequently operate out of a sense of fear of losing control, status, or power. A political dictator normally spends an excessive amount of time and effort maintaining his position of power.

FIGURE 2
Aggressive and Submissive Leadership Styles

Excessively aggressive leaders have a strong tendency to substitute their personal goals, or goals that seem right to them, for the goals of the group. Autocrats do not typically think of helping the group to achieve its goals, because the autocrats believe that they know best what is good for their followers, or in the case of spiritual leaders, what the will of God is for the church. Autocrats feel their goals are superior to those formed by the participative action of the group.

Of course, it may be true that the leader knows best. However, spiritual leaders must be careful about deciding what is best for other people unless such decisions are clearly based upon the Word of God. There is great danger of self-deception. Leaders frequently are deceived into thinking that what they want is the will of God.

Aggressive behavior is pressure by leaders to accomplish their objectives. All overt persuasion is aggressive to various degrees, but as aggressive behavior is increased in an effort to control, there is an increasing likelihood that the leaders will use unethical or manipulative methods (or methods perceived as manipulative) to enforce their will. An autocratic leader is tempted to believe that the end justifies whatever means it takes to get his goals accomplished, particularly as the goals become increasingly important in the leader's mind. When a leader is absolutely confident that a certain action must be taken by followers, he is tempted to distort facts, bribe followers (maybe only with a cup of coffee), or in various ways domineer constituents and behave unethically. Every leader must realize that few things are more fatal to effective spiritual leadership than unethical or manipulative conduct.

The primary external indication of autocratic behavior is an attempt to control the group and dominate the decision-making process to ensure the enactment of the leader's will. The primary internal indication of autocracy is an attitude of superiority or lack of trust in members of the group. In lesser forms of aggressiveness, these things may not be true, or they may be true to a lesser degree. It is reasonable to suggest, however, that as aggressiveness increases these qualities become more obvious.

Yet, there are times and situations when aggressiveness is necessary and these dangers must be faced. A father, for example, should know that he must be very controlling of his two-year-old, but as the child matures and becomes capable of making decisions, the father must become less controlling. Fathers who attempt to control a seventeen-year-old like a two-year-old usually encounter resistance or rebellion.

In other words, a moral judgment should not be passed on aggressive leadership per se, except, perhaps, in its most extreme form of totalitarian control. Rather, two questions should be asked: What degree of aggressiveness is called for in a given situation, and how can that aggressiveness be carried out ethically?

Submissive Leadership Behavior

Submissive leadership behavior is here described in its extreme form. Submissiveness, like aggressiveness, is a matter of degree, and a good leader may at times be quite submissive without exhibiting some of the following traits.

Submissive leaders are generally convinced that better decisions are made by the whole group working and cooperating together. There is considerable trust in the wisdom of others, and there is confidence that the group will normally make the best decision possible.[2] Of course, such confidence is sometimes misguided, and the group may not be worthy of such trust or capable of making good decisions.

Submissive leaders refuse to dominate or control group decisions, particularly decisions on issues in which the leaders have no special expertise. Rather, nonaggressive leaders generally regard their responsibilities as those of stimulating discussion, coordinating group activities, and guiding the process. Of course, submissiveness in its most extreme form is nonparticipation in the process, a virtual abdication of the leadership role.

Submissive behavior indicates an ability to accept the decisions of others. Such leaders may be secure enough not to feel threatened or personally rejected if their opinions do not prevail. Submissiveness may be an indication that the leader believes that decisions made by the whole body are owned by the people and, therefore, are more easily and effectively implemented.

Submissive leaders tend to be conscientious in refusing to manipulate people. The danger, however, is that in its extreme form such conscientious behavior may simply be withdrawal from the

2. That groups normally make better decisions than individuals, except when the individual possesses expertise on a given subject, is well established in research literature.

responsibilities of leadership. There is obviously great difficulty in rejecting an attitude of superiority and respecting the opinions of others, while at the same time being sufficiently aggressive to actively fulfill the responsibilites of leadership. A submissive leader may be weak or cowardly, not merely conscientious.

Participatory leaders (who exhibit a moderate form of submissiveness) tend to see themselves as members of the group; as members of the group, they participate in group discussions and decision making without attempting to control the group. They feel free, as do others, to state their opinions and argue for them with facts and sincere emotion. Such leaders are marked by a deep internal conviction that others have valuable insights and contributions to make. Such leaders' external efforts are largely concentrated in securing the whole group's participation in setting and achieving group goals.[3]

Different people have different ideas about what degree of leadership aggressiveness is better than another. Probably, however, no style is better than another, but one style is better suited to a given situation than another. Wise leaders adjust their styles to fit each occasion, sometimes being assertive and sometimes being participatory. This leads to a discussion of the relationship between leadership style and effectiveness.

Style and Effectiveness

Typically, aggressiveness is associated with effectiveness, and submissiveness is associated with ineffectiveness. Aggressive or dominating leaders are regarded as strong leaders, and nonaggressive or submissive leaders are thought of as weak leaders. Such thinking, however, is incorrect. Sometimes, the more submissive leader is far more influential and effective than the aggressive leader. The submissive leader is often the strong leader, and the aggressive leader is often the weak leader, as measured in terms of leader influence or group achievement.

The degree of aggressiveness is not related to the degree of influence brought to bear in a given situation. This is crucial for

3. The classic definition of participatory leadership is found in Thomas Gordon's two excellent books, *Group-Centered Leadership* (Boston: Houghton Mifflin, 1955) and *Leader Effectiveness Training* (New York: Wyden, 1977).

leaders to know, for leaders are tempted to think that to be effective or influential they must be aggressive or dominating. Yet, extremely autocratic behavior can be devoid of real influence, while submissive behavior can be influential.

How can this be? Effectiveness is determined more by the ethos (perceived credibility) and competence of the leaders, and by group ability and motivation, than by aggressive leadership behavior. A leader may be extremely aggressive in behavior, but be perceived as a blundering idiot or an obnoxious potentate. Such a leader's real influence is usually negligible, unless people are abnormally submissive and weak. On the other hand, leaders may be quite submissive in their style, but be influential because they are perceived as trustworthy and wise.

An example may be helpful. Suppose a church or church board must make an important decision involving a matter of finances. One of the trustees, Bruce, is a godly, highly respected, and competent certified public accountant, a successful manager of his own business. As the discussion is carried out, he chooses merely to listen and perhaps to ask a few intelligent questions. Finally, someone asks, "I would like to ask Bruce what he thinks we should do." Bruce responds, "Well, I certainly don't have a corner on wisdom, and I'm willing to accept the decision of the group. I guess, however, if you really pinned me down, I think it might be better to choose Plan B rather than one of the other suggestions. Plan B seems to be more fiscally sound and compatible with our goals than other plans." This is not aggressive behavior, yet because of the profound respect the group has for him and his competence in matters of finance, it is likely that his opinion will influence the decision.

The opposite is likewise true. Suppose, using the same scenario, that an official with no particular reputation for godliness, wisdom, or fiscal knowledge speaks up in an authoritative tone: "What this group is considering is stupid. You had better choose Plan A or you're making a serious mistake. You will miss the will of God for our church unless you do what I think is best." Obviously, this is extremely aggressive behavior. The group, however, is likely to have little respect for such a person, may resent his attempts to control the decision, and discount his aggressive efforts. He is not influential, despite his aggressiveness, except perhaps to influence the group in the opposite direction.

Style is not necessarily related to the degree of influence brought to bear. A reasonably aggressive style, when coupled with a reputation for integrity and graciousness, may be effective by many standards and in many situations.

Dangers of Inappropriate Style

Two preliminary truths should be noted before discussing the dangers of incorrectly choosing one's leadership style. First, the question is never either-or, either aggressive or submissive. Flexibility is essential in leadership. Leaders must allow themselves considerable latitude of actions with which they are comfortable in varying circumstances. They should be willing to use different styles or different degrees of aggressiveness or submissiveness when the circumstances call for them. Sometimes it is necessary to behave in an uncharacteristic manner for the sake of efficiency or effectiveness.

Second, neither extreme is particularly desirable or effective for spiritual leaders, and extreme autocracy is biblically prohibited. Effective leaders tend to be participatory or mildly aggressive. In the business world this truth is well-documented: "The more successful companies have been those whose management can be characterized by a balanced, participative style that encourages maximum participation while discouraging permissiveness."[4] It seems that this may also be true in spiritual leadership.

When leaders choose certain behaviors, more aggressive or more submissive, they should be aware of the ramifications of repeated errors in those choices. People will eventually depose leaders whose judgment is poor and whose leadership style is not appropriate for the situation. Many church leaders have lost the opportunity to be effective because they have erred repeatedly by choosing a style of leadership inappropriate for the circumstances. No amount of theological or theoretical knowledge will compensate for lack of common sense and discerning judgment in making right choices in leadership style. Three factors highlight the need for leaders to develop good judgment in making choices.

4. Dale McConkey, *How to Manage by Results* (New York: American Management Associations, 1983), 5.

Undermined Confidence

Leaders who behave inappropriately in their attempts to influence will lose credibility, and nothing is more important to successful leadership than credibility. When leaders are excessively aggressive they may be perceived as dictators. If leaders are inappropriately and repeatedly submissive, it is likely that they will be perceived as weak or as nonleaders.

Dictators may succeed in dominating submissive followers and building impressive organizations, but this does not make them successful leaders by biblical criteria. Laissez-faire leaders may be dearly loved by their followers, but this does not mean that other worthwhile objectives are achieved.

Lack of Achievement

Submissive leaders tend to err in their excessive concern for congeniality and harmony, which often results in the absence of task fulfillment; nonaggressive church leaders sometimes become compulsive about achieving cohesiveness. Such leaders fail to see other, equally important tasks and, in their desire to avoid controversy, they do not stimulate group achievement. If followers become restless about the stagnation of the group, submissive behavior may also eventually result in the lack of harmony that these leaders so desperately desire.

Servility or Hostility

Leadership behavior that errs toward too much control may well result in either a servile submissiveness or hostility (or both) in the attitudes of followers. An excessively aggressive leader may achieve some worthy goals, but group submissiveness may make leadership development difficult or impossible. And as Kenneth O. Gangel correctly observes, "Good leadership always breeds leadership."[5] Also, aggressive leadership behavior may provoke open antagonism, sullen silence, or quiet withdrawal—all expressions of hostility. Many people resist the autocratic behavior of others.

The fundamental assumption in leadership behavior is that it is wise for a leader to be no more aggressive than it is absolutely necessary to be. Further, even when aggressive behavior seems justifiable, the conduct of the leader must be gracious, winsome,

5. Kenneth O. Gangel, *Competent to Lead* (Chicago: Moody, 1974), 47.

and respectful of the opinions of others. The haughtiness, superiority, and ungraciousness often associated with autocracy are always out of order in spiritual leadership. When the leader's character, reputation, and wisdom are truly evident, he need not be unduly aggressive to be influential.

Guidelines for Leadership Style

The discussion about the dangers of inappropriate style leads us back to two crucial questions: What aspects of a situation help the leader to make decisions about leadership style? Are there guidelines that can direct leaders in their decisions about leadership style?

Fundamental is the premise that spiritual leaders have a passionate desire to help others achieve worthy goals. Good leaders make decisions about their leadership style with a conscious desire to minister to the needs of others and a genuine concern for their welfare.

> Leaders who do the best job are those whose antennae are keenly attuned to others. They sense the scene, they get the picture, they read between the lines. And having done so, they operate from that sensitive vantage point, which weaves wisdom and understanding into the fabric of their leadership. Those who respond to such leaders do so with delight because they realize their leader cares . . . cares about them personally.[6]

In a caring ministry, leaders must be aggressive at some times and submissive at other times. Spiritual leaders can use six considerations to guide their decisions about leadership style.

The Type of Task or Issue

There are basically two kinds of tasks or issues. The first type of task is sometimes spoken of as a problem-solving task. When decisions are made about this type of task, people are not likely to become emotionally distraught or offended if things do not go their way. The second type of task is often referred to as a policy-making task. People are likely to feel deeply about this type of task and may become angry or hurt when their ideas do not prevail.

6. Charles Swindoll, *Leadership* (Waco: Word, 1985), 52.

Churches split over policy-making issues; seldom is there much disruption over problem-solving tasks.

The crucial principle is that policy-making issues require a participatory style of leadership. There are several reasons for this, but the most important is that decisions involving values require consensus and, therefore, more involvement of people in the decision-making process.

A problem-solving decision may usually be made by a simple majority vote without seriously disrupting the unity of the church, because objective facts, not subjective feelings, are uppermost in these decisions. A policy-making decision that involves the value systems of many people cannot usually be made successfully by simple majority vote. A greater consensus is necessary to preserve the cohesiveness of the group: the stronger the value systems, the greater the consensus needed. For policy-making tasks the most important data to be considered are the value systems of the people most directly affected by the decision.

Church leaders make serious errors when they fail to discern the value systems and emotional involvement of the people affected by a decision. When policy-making issues are decided by the aggressive action of leaders without allowing group participation in the decision-making process, the disaster of disunity is not far away; or to put it bluntly, a battle may be won while the war is lost. The goal of good leaders is to help accomplish goals while maintaining group solidarity.

This aspect of leadership is complicated, because what may be a simple problem-solving task for one person may be a policy-making task for another. Further, not many issues are wholly problem-solving or wholly policy-making. The lines dividing them are not sharp or readily discernible. It takes a wise, spiritually discerning leader to correctly evaluate these matters and adjust style accordingly. There are no guarantees of success.

Degree of Importance

Excellent leaders always evaluate the importance of issues facing the church and its groups. Wise leaders recognize that many decisions are inconsequential and others are crucial. The best leaders understand the relative importance of tasks, issues, and decisions.

Two behavioral principles flow from the degree of importance of the issue. First, unimportant issues usually justify submissiveness in leadership style. This is only logical. To be dominant and aggressive on unimportant issues is to risk provoking hostility or servility among followers when, in fact, the decision doesn't matter that much. There is always risk in aggressive behavior, and few things are more obviously foolish than attempts to control inconsequential decisions. Someone has wisely said, "Choose carefully the hills [issues] upon which you wish to die." To take a hard line or to be excessively aggressive on trivial issues is a serious error often made by poor leaders.

Second, important issues may necessitate an assertive style of behavior. The good leader cannot afford to be laissez-faire or too submissive when the issue is vital, unless, perhaps, an acceptable decision is already assured through the leadership of others or through the obvious maturity of the group. If the group has a record of making excellent decisions, the leader may decide to be nonaggressive because he has confidence in the ability of the group.

Good leaders will not always be aggressive on important issues; they weigh carefully many facts and answer some intelligent questions. What is the likelihood that a poor decision (not merely one unacceptable to the leader) will be made if the leaders take no aggressive stance? What degree of aggressive behavior will other leaders take? Are the people making the decision likely to yield to aggressive leadership behavior or are they likely to rebel? (This depends mostly on the esteem or affection which the group members feel for the leader.) What are the expected results of a decision that differs from the leader's opinion? What facts are available upon which to base the need for aggressive behavior?

An example may be helpful. Suppose the issue is important, perhaps involving a major Christian doctrine. There is little Christian maturity in the group; there is solid scriptural evidence regarding the issue; and the group highly esteems the leaders. The following factors must be considered:

1. The issue is important since it involves a crucial doctrine of the church.
2. Scripture is clear on this subject, and leaders will have objective, exegetical evidence in support of their position.
3. There is little maturity in the church and therefore a poor decision is possible, or maybe even likely, without aggressive leadership.

4. The consequences of a poor decision would be disastrous.
5. People who esteem leaders highly are apt to tolerate (and even desire) their aggressive influence and guidance. Resentment is not anticipated.

With this configuration of circumstances, aggressive leadership is necessary. It should be blended with the graciousness that characterizes all spiritual leadership.

There is always the danger of self-deception or poor judgment on the leader's part. Leaders may believe something is important when it is not—a mistake frequently made. Leaders may think aggressive behavior will be tolerated when it may not be. Leaders may trust others to lead correctly when they will not. Judgment—the ability to discern these things and adjust one's behavior accordingly—separates good leaders from poor ones, and is an indispensable ingredient of good leadership. Some leaders never gain this kind of common sense; they repeat their mistakes in leadership style throughout their lifetime.

Availability of Data

Two behavioral principles are determined by the availability of data. First, absence of facts calls for submissive behavior. Again, this is obvious. To be assertive and controlling when one does not have the facts necessary to support one's position is absurd. Few things will cause loss of credibility faster than to speak forcefully, but in ignorance about the issue at hand.

For example, a pastor may be theologically competent but relatively uneducated about matters of budget, debt ceilings, or investments. For such a pastor to be aggressive in financial matters with a group of trustees who have expertise in these things is foolish. For anyone to be dominating in matters outside his or her area of expertise is to risk appearing irresponsible and reckless. Loss of credibility is assured if there is only heat and no light, opinion but no facts.

Second, possession of facts may justify aggressive behavior. A wise leader who speaks logically, clearly, forcefully, graciously, and with obvious expertise is rarely resented.

Efficiency Requirements

Again, two behavioral principles may be determined by efficiency requirements. First, the need for efficiency may require aggressive behavior, particularly with problem-solving issues. Many issues simply do not require group discussion, and good leaders are conscious of the dangers of wasting time.

An airline captain in an emergency may find it necessary to make immediate and unilateral decisions. Maybe better decisions could be made through group process and consultation with other pilots, air-control personnel, and aircraft technicians. But in an emergency, time is of the essence, and efficiency demands aggressive, even autocratic, behavior. In such cases, urgency becomes a controlling factor in leadership style, and it is hoped that the captain has sufficient experience and wisdom to make the right decision.

Spiritual leaders however, need to accurately determine if issues justify aggressive or unilateral behavior. Impatience with group process may cause leaders to claim urgency when none exists. Autocratic church leaders may claim that considerations of efficiency justify their leadership style. Nothing is quite as efficient as a dictatorship, but the obvious dangers of abuse must not be overlooked.

Second, when the need for quality in decision making eclipses the need for efficiency, participatory behavior is usually wise. Individuals make quick decisions, and sometimes quick decisions are necessary. However, groups normally make better decisions, particularly on policy-making issues, and when the need for a better decision is crucial, a good leader slows down, stimulates participation of the people affected, promotes debate, and utilizes healthy group process. In these situations, good leaders are not unduly aggressive or controlling; they are participative in style.

Leadership Vacuum

Again, there are two primary considerations. First, the availability of other competent leadership makes aggressive behavior unnecessary. When there are people who are able, willing, and in position to offer leadership, other leaders may choose to be quite laissez-faire, particularly in areas outside their areas of expertise. Such leaders may wisely defer to the leadership of others.

Second, a leadership vacuum in the group may necessitate aggressive behavior. Groups seldom make good decisions (or any decisions) without leadership. To avoid the drifting and the lack of action that accompany leadership vacuum, the good leader often finds it necessary to be aggressive in style.

For example, pastors may find it necessary to be uncharacteristically aggressive if they serve young churches full of new Christians and devoid of mature leaders. As leaders are trained and become competent, those pastors usually find it wise to be less assertive in many areas, spending their time and effort on other matters that need their attention. Paul was very assertive with his young churches, but it is difficult to believe that he would be equally dominating with mature, wise Christians.

Group Cohesiveness

Lack of group cohesiveness often necessitates a participatory style in leadership because, normally, a participatory style promotes unity. On the other hand, when there is group solidarity, leaders often may be aggressive without fear of resentment, providing the leaders are highly esteemed by their constituency. Normally (but not always), church cohesiveness is more important than any possible decision on an issue. The loss of church unity is disastrous to public testimony and to interpersonal relationships.

It is interesting to note that great biblical leaders were flexible in their leadership style, sometimes aggressive and sometimes laissez-faire. Jesus was aggressive in cleansing the temple, but refused to be dominant on other occasions. Similarly, Paul was assertive on occasions, particularly when he was confident of God's will, as in moral matters, but he was quite nonaggressive on other occasions of lesser importance.

The preceding suggestions are guidelines for choosing suitable leadership behavior. The guidelines are compatible with leadership behavior in the New Testament. Jesus authoritatively cleansed the temple because the issue was important, he possessed facts ("It is written"), efficiency required it, and there was a leadership vacuum. These factors outweighed others that might have caused him to be more passive. Similarly, Paul was assertive in his counsel to the church at Corinth because the issues were important, he was certain of the facts, the church lacked maturity, and there was a leadership vacuum. The elders and apostles were participative at the Jerusalem council because the issues involved cherished values, a consensus was needed, and unity needed to be preserved.

The critical factor is flexibility. Sometimes a good leader becomes participative, even submissive, in leadership efforts. Sometimes an aggressive stance is required.

> Followers do like being treated with consideration, do like to have their say, do like a chance to exercise their own initiative—and participation does increase acceptance of decisions. But there are times when followers welcome rather than reject authority, want prompt and clear decisions from the leader, want to close ranks around the leader. The ablest and most effective leaders do not hold to a single style; they may be highly supportive in personal relations when that is needed, yet capable of a quick authoritative decision when the situation requires it.[7]

Summary

The question of leadership behavior is one of style along a continuum from laissez-faire to autocratic. The critical question is to what extent and in what manner should leaders influence or attempt to influence the decisions of the church and its boards and committees? There are no perfect answers.

The typical characteristics of autocrats are feelings of superiority, lack of trust or confidence in others, attempts to control the decision-making process, difficulty in yielding to the opinions of others, substitution of leaders' goals for group goals, and, sometimes, manipulative tactics to gain power over followers. Spiritual leaders who tend toward aggressiveness must recognize these dangers of their style.

Submissive or participatory leaders tend to trust the opinions and decisions of others, refuse to dominate or control, encourage dissent and debate, believe group decisions are group owned and more easily implemented, help groups set their own goals, and see themselves as participating members within the group. However, submissive leaders may be merely weak or timid, and leaders who tend toward submissiveness must recognize the dangers inherent in their style.

Good leaders are always flexible, adjusting leadership behavior according to the situation. Good leaders tend to be aggressive when the issue is important, when data are available, when efficiency

7. John W. Gardner, *The Heart of the Matter: Leader-Constituent Interaction* (Washington, D.C.: Independent Sector, 1986), 8.

demands it, when there is a leadership vacuum, and when the group is cohesive. On the other hand, good leaders tend to be participative when issues involve values or are unimportant, when data are unavailable, when considered decisions are more important than quick decisions, when the group is mature, when other competent leadership is available, and when the group is not cohesive.

Continual use of authoritarian methods is inconsistent with scriptural guidelines for spiritual servant-leadership, for church leaders are not to be "lords." When reasonably aggressive behavior is justified, it must be accompanied by graciousness and respect for the opinion of others. Autocratic behavior of leaders on policy-making issues is especially dangerous. Achievement of consensus, especially on sensitive policy-making matters, should be a major goal of good spiritual leaders.

6

The Delicacy of Leadership *Balance*

The problems of leadership style are numerous, confusing, and complicated. One of the principles governing a leader's adjustment of style is frequently in conflict with another principle and the leader must weigh the relative merits of each guideline.

For example, policy-making issues generally need a participatory style of leadership to gain a consensus; yet, policy-making issues are almost always important issues, and important issues frequently call for assertive action from leaders. The two guidelines work against each other; therefore, the leader is forced to choose between leadership styles.

There are many other similar difficulties and pitfalls for leaders who strive to be flexible, and even the most mature leaders will make mistakes. Nevertheless, understanding the general guidelines and tensions in leadership style is crucial if errors in leadership style are to be minimized.

One of the fundamental questions of leadership style has to do with authority. How much authority does a spiritual leader have? Scripture teaches that no one except Christ himself is the head of the body and organization that is the church. Certainly no one man ruled the local church in New Testament times. The idea of one man assuming control over the church grew slowly throughout the ante-Nicene era:

> Gradually the principal officiant at the cultural re-enactment of the Supper came to be so closely associated with Christ . . . in the sacrifice of Calvary and its liturgical commemoration, the Eucharist, that by contagion and imputation the eucharistic president himself became looked upon as at least analogous to the high priest of the Old Covenant and the spokesman of the entire royal priesthood which is the Church. Though he was normally one of the presbyters, the cultural president acquired, through his supervision of the deacons, a pre-eminence over the other presbyters in their corporate capacity as the "municipal" council of Christians whose ultimate citizenship was in heaven.[1]

Eventually this trend led to the excesses of priesthood and popery. The time came when kings had to check with Rome before exercising power or making key decisions. Preachers never played God more effectively than in the Middle Ages: "Preachers told kings when they could go to war and which wars were holy. Preachers told scholars what they might study and what could not be examined. Preachers told lenders what was reasonable interest on a loan and what was exorbitant. Preachers told powerful men whom they might marry and if they might get a divorce."[2] These excesses of leadership authority have become obvious to us, yet there is still difficulty in achieving an appropriate, biblical balance.

What are some of the tensions of leadership style? How do good leaders manage the tensions, balance their priorities, and minimize their mistakes? As in so many areas of life, balance, especially balance in biblical interpretation of texts pertinent to authority and leadership orientation, is essential.

1. H. Richard Niebuhr and Daniel D. Williams, eds., *The Ministry in Historical Perspective* (New York: Harper and Brothers, 1956), 28.
2. Claude A. Frazier, *Should Preachers Play God?* (Independence, Mo.: Independence Press, 1973), 13.

Balance in Biblical Interpretation

Authoritarian leaders tend to emphasize one biblical teaching at the expense of another. Some denominations have probably emphasized leadership authority too much, and their leaders have been invested with excessive authority, an authority without checks that becomes too easy to abuse. Similarly, submissive leaders tend to focus on one scriptural truth and neglect another. Some denominations have not emphasized leadership authority sufficiently, and their leaders have been crippled, unable to lead.

The Bible has much to say about the qualities of character necessary for spiritual leadership, but it says comparatively little about a leader's specific duties or authority. The New Testament speaks of the spiritual leader's responsibilities only in generalities: "take care of God's church" (1 Tim. 3:5) and "direct the affairs of the church" (1 Tim. 5:17). There has been wide divergence in Christianity in the specific applications of these broad truths. Some differences of opinion are healthy but caution must be taken against being overly dogmatic about any individual viewpoint. God raises up people with different opinions and different styles of leadership to suit various situations, and care must be taken to avoid being judgmental of those who differ; yet, we must not excuse either incompetence or the self-will that characterizes many leaders.

The biblical authors never gave a systematic treatment of the limitations of leadership authority. Nowhere in Scripture is there a clear and unequivocal statement of the appropriate use of leadership authority, exactly how much authority leaders have, and in exactly what decisions that authority should be exercised.

However, we are not left without biblical guidance in these matters. A delicate balance between two equally clear lines of biblical teaching must be maintained. The church's leaders are to be overseers, but not lords over God's heritage. The church is to obey and submit, but is not to be blindly obeisant or servile. Leaders are not to dominate and control church decisions or the personal lives of members, but neither is the church to be hostile and resistant to the counsel of its leaders.

The church is advised to obey its leaders, but it is also instructed to "test everything" (1 Thess. 5:21) and "watch out for those who cause divisions and put obstacles in your way" (Rom. 16:17). While the church and its members must not be recalcitrant, the church must be spiritually discerning and "test the spirits to see whether they are from God, because many false prophets have gone out into the world" (1 John 4:1). The church must be spiritually discerning enough to reject the counsel of its leaders when that counsel is wrong. It is unrealistic to think that spiritual leaders are always right or that responsible positions are always filled by wise leaders.

For their part, leaders have the authority of overseers, examples, teachers, and guides, but none of this gives them license to be dictators or "lord it over" (1 Pet. 5:3; Greek *katakurieuo*) the church.

The church has always struggled with these truths, and today's church is no exception. An appropriate balance is essential, but it is not easy to attain. Many leaders err—some toward autocracy, others toward servility. Many churches err—some toward blind deference to leaders, others toward disrespect or defiance of leaders.

What is the proper balance of leader authority and follower submission? How do leaders behave in a manner that does not abuse their privilege, and how do followers behave in a manner that properly respects spiritual authority? Certain truths are unmistakable in Scripture. Two lines of truth must be emphasized and carefully balanced.

Leaders Are Granted Authority

Scripture does emphasize the authority of spiritual leadership in the church. It is impossible to discern a pure democracy in the church of the first century. The idea that all decisions of any consequence must be submitted to congregational vote, or that congregations should maintain veto power over all leadership decisions is simply not to be found in the New Testament. Our culture's commitment to political democracy has influenced church opinion in this matter, particularly in congregational ecclesiology.[3] Each Christian must live in a community of believers and under the discipline of scripturally constituted authority in the body. Leaders must be selected and trusted with responsibility. Members are to respect leadership authority, and leaders are expected to act within carefully stipulated guidelines.

One of the primary emphases of the Reformation was the priest-

3. Of course, not even the most vigorous defenders of congregationalism actually operate in the church as a pure democracy.

hood of the believer, which denies the right of mediatorship between God and man to any human leader. Modern-day reformers have carried this truth to the extreme by disavowing any distinction between leaders and followers, virtually erasing the significance of leadership, ordination, and the distinct gifts and calling of spiritual leaders. As a result, ecclesiastical authority has eroded notably throughout Christendom.

The priesthood of the believer does not eliminate the authority of scriptural leaders, nor does it reduce the responsibility of church members to submit to such properly constituted authority in the church. People err if they use the cherished doctrine of the believer's priesthood as justification for an independent spirit or resistance to church leaders. Never has it been acceptable for church members to ignore or disregard the spiritual counsel of the church's leaders.

Some leaders of strong or charismatic personality have resisted the modern trend toward insubordination and have become autocrats (usually benevolent) who hold excessive decision-making power in their churches. Many others attempt to be autocrats with disastrous results. At the other extreme, some churches are crippled because they refuse to delegate any authority to their leaders.

New Testament leaders were selected, elected, or appointed (the method probably varied) and they were given the responsibility of administering the affairs of the church within certain limitations. The degree of their authority in directing the church is not specified and undoubtedly differed from church to church. Those not selected for leadership were to obey and submit to their spiritual leaders.

Multiple leaders, sharing more or less equally the burdens of spiritual oversight, were the norm in New Testament churches. This was apparently a safeguard against abuses of leadership authority.[4]

These primary passages emphasize leadership authority:

Now we ask you, brothers, to respect those who work hard among you, who are over you in the Lord and who admonish you. Hold them in the highest regard in love, because of their work. [1 Thess. 5:12–13]

4. For an exposition of the subject of multiple spiritual leadership in the church, see Robert Saucy, *The Church in God's Program* (Chicago: Moody, 1972).

The elders who direct the affairs of the church well are worthy of double honor, especially those whose work is preaching and teaching. [1 Tim. 5:17]

Obey your leaders and submit to their authority. They keep watch over you as men who must give an account. Obey them so that their work will be a joy, not a burden, for that would be of no advantage to you. [Heb. 13:17]

I will give you the keys of the kingdom of heaven; whatever you bind on earth will be bound in heaven, and whatever you loose on earth will be loosed in heaven. [Matt. 16:19]

Clearly, leaders were over the church and the church was under that authority. No one had the right to disregard or disrespect the spiritual leaders. A safe assumption is that this respect was called for only when leaders did not abuse their power or position. Leaders who lose respect deserve to lose authority because of their unwise or unspiritual use of that authority, or because they exhibit unspiritual behavior in their personal lives.

Scripture makes clear that leaders are to direct the affairs of the church and the church is to honor its leaders. A cavalier attitude that casually dismisses the direction of the elders and that refuses them due honor is not to be tolerated.

The strong words of admonition to the church are *obey* and *submit*. Scripture does not give an extensive list of situations in which church members are to submit to leaders, but it seems safe to conclude that situations involving spiritual matters in the corporate body are inferred.

It is generally agreed that leaders do not have any authority over the personal lives of church members except to insist upon basic, biblical standards of moral conduct and decency, as did the apostle Paul with the church at Corinth.

Individual churches differ on exactly what standards constitute a "covenant" and what the sanctions are for violation of the accepted code of conduct. There are some notorious cases of abuse in churches in which leaders have totally dominated the personal lives of followers. Such leaders become gurus; tragedy usually follows.[5]

While interpretations of Matthew 16:18 vary widely according to church ecclesiology, it cannot be denied that Peter was granted

_____

5. James Jones and the tragedy in Guyana is a case in point.

some significant authority in the church. It is debatable to what extent this authroity was intended to apply to successive genera-tions of church leaders. However, even though apostolic succession may be denied, most biblical scholars agree that the church's lead-ers were granted positions of considerable authority as God's spokesmen on earth.

The preceding passages indicate that spiritual leaders (particu-larly elders) are to be accorded a special esteem, a place of honor, respect, and deference in the church. The passages do not imply that leaders have a right to be authoritarian or high-handed; yet, leaders are not to be seen as merely one voice among many. Lead-ers have "a noble task" (1 Tim. 3:1); they are "entrusted with God's work" (Titus 1:7), which is distinct in form, function, and authority from other work in the church.

Care must be taken, however, to emphasize that the leaders' position does not imply superiority in the economy of God. In no sense are elders superior to others in the church; in no sense are followers inferior to leaders. No position of leadership justifies an attitude that the leader enjoys a special status with God and fol-lowers are lesser beings in God's program. Diotrophes "love[d] to be first" (3 John 9), but he was rejected as a leader in the church. His very desire for preeminence disqualified him from leadership. Each member has an important function in the body and "those parts of the body that seem to be weaker are indispensable" (1 Cor. 12:22).

Leaders Are Servants, Not Lords

Never are church leaders to think of their status as lordship, but as servanthood. Leaders are not selected so that they might have dominion over the body of believers, but that there might be guid-ance in spiritual matters by qualified, godly individuals under the lordship of Christ. Therefore, however we interpret the words *rule*, *direct*, *obey*, and *submit*, they cannot be interpreted in a way that gives leaders the kind of authority that the rulers of the Gentiles had, or that high officials exercise in the secular world.

Jesus magnified the concept of service, not authority. Leaders are leaders because they are excellent servants, not powerful rulers.

Jesus' view of service grows out of the Old Testament command of love for one's neighbor, which He takes and links with the command of love for God to constitute the substance of the divinely willed

ethical conduct of his followers. In so doing, He purifies the concept
of service from the distortions which it suffered in Judaism. Jesus'
attitude to service is completely new as compared with the Greek
understanding. The decisive point is that He sees it in the thing
which makes a man His disciple.[6]

Spiritual leaders are always servant-leaders. Three primary passages emphasize this dimension of leadership:

> Be shepherds of God's flock that is under your care, serving as over-
> seers—not because you must, but because you are willing, as God
> wants you to be; not greedy for money, but eager to serve; not
> lording it over those entrusted to you, but being examples to the
> flock. [1 Pet. 5:2–3]

> "You know that the rulers of the Gentiles lord it over them, and their
> high officials exercise authority over them. Not so with you. Instead,
> whoever wants to become great among you must be your servant,
> and whoever wants to be first must be your slave—just as the Son
> of Man did not come to be served, but to serve, and to give his life
> as a ransom for many." [Matt. 20:25–28]

> "You call me 'Teacher' and 'Lord,' and rightly so, for that is what I
> am. Now that I, your Lord and Teacher, have washed your feet, you
> also should wash one another's feet. I have set you an example that
> you should do as I have done for you." [John 13:13–15]

The emphasis should be upon the words *eager to serve*. The
words *lording it over* refer to a dominating, dictatorial, arrogant
spirit commonly found in secular leaders, but intolerable in spiritual leaders.

Christ insisted that leadership in the church is distinctly different from the kind of leadership found among unbelievers. Greatness in leadership means greatness in service, not greatness in
being served. A biblical leader can be characterized not as a com-
mander served by subordinates, but as a mother or a father caring
for and dealing with her or his children (see 1 Thess. 2:7, 11).

True leadership requires service that is often considered routine
or menial. The symbol of leadership is not the scepter, but the

6. Gerhard Kittel, ed., *Theological Dictionary of the New Testament* (Grand Rapids:
Eerdmans, 1964), 2:84.

towel. True spiritual leaders never think of themselves as authority figures, only as servants.

These passages, along with others, teach that leadership authority in the church is something much different from what is commonly found in business or politics. Duly functioning spiritual leaders do not dominate; they serve. Spiritual leaders do not command; they guide. Christian leaders do not manipulate; they teach. Church leaders do not subjugate; they inspire. Real spiritual leaders are not lords; they are models and ministers. Whenever these truths are forgotten or ignored, church leaders become dictators, overbearing and ugly:

> A little Protestant despot, a petty parochial pope, is a sorry caricature of a minister of Jesus Christ. A minister who boasts under his breath that he proposes to run things and who chuckles at his adeptness in manipulating people, and who says by his manner that he is the boss of the parish is a man who is a stumbling-block in the way of Christian progress.[7]

When leaders become concerned with who's in charge they are disqualified for leadership and churches must reject them. Good, spiritual leaders never seek power over people; they seek to serve their constituents. Kenneth O. Gangel is correct when he says, "To put it simply, Christian leadership is not authoritative control over the minds and behavior of other people."[8]

Love of preeminence, greatness, and authority is the antithesis of biblical leadership. Excellence in service gives credence to the power of example. Leadership style was never meant to be developed along the lines of personal magnetism or charisma, but according to spiritual power and divine grace.

The economy of the church is such that leaders and followers alike must recognize the parallel lines of scriptural truth. The church must respect the position and authority of its leaders and, without groveling, be willing to yield the right to lead. Leaders must constantly remind themselves that they are servants of the church; their power is the power of example, teacher, and servant. Such power does not give them the right to insist upon their own way

7. Charles Jefferson, *The Ministering Shepherd* (Paris: Young Men's Christian Association, 1912), 72.
8. Kenneth O. Gangel, *Competent to Lead* (Chicago: Moody, 1974), 12.

or to demand that their personal opinions be enacted as church decisions.

The real power of leaders is the Word of God spoken through them and exemplified in them. The church is commanded to obey and submit; however, obedience and submission are not to the whims or edicts of the leaders themselves or even to their considered opinions, but to the Word of God taught through them. It is questionable whether spiritual leaders have any authority other than the Word faithfully declared and exemplified.[9] The church, however, may willingly defer to the carefully considered convictions of its leaders, not because of their authority, but because of their demonstrated wisdom and spiritual maturity.

The direction given by elders is that of those who preside, or who give spiritual oversight as fathers, not the ruling power of legislators or executors.[10] As Thomas Coates has written, "This does not imply any personal authority on the part of the minister, but rather refers to his responsibility as spiritual watchman over the flock. As such he is entitled to respect. Obedience is due to the Word which the minister proclaims, not to his person."[11]

There is a constant danger of imbalance. Leaders are in danger of abusing their authority; yet they cannot become obsequious in their ministries. Followers must not reject the guidance of their leaders, but neither should their submission become mindless obeisance to leadership's whims or excesses.

Leaders can speak with absolute authority only when they declare the will of God revealed in Scripture, but there is the constant danger of leaders believing that the will of God is what they want the church to do. One of the temptations of leadership is self-deception, which entices leaders to substitute their personal desires for the will of God. The function of leadership is to model, teach, inspire, motivate, and guide the church in its corporate life, not to inflict its own will upon the congregation.

9. For an excellent discussion of leadership authority as it developed in the New Testament and through church history, see David A. Steele, *Images of Leadership and Authority for the Church* (New York: University Press of America, 1986), 3–64.

10. The word translated "direct" in 1 Timothy 5:17 and "over you" in 1 Thessalonians 5:12 is the Greek word *proistēmi*, to preside. Paul uses it also in 1 Timothy 3:4, 5, 12 of fathers who care properly for their families.

11. Thomas Coates, *Authority in the Church* (St. Louis: Concordia, 1964), 49.

A Balance in Basic Orientation

Leaders tend to fall into one of two basic categories. They tend to be either task oriented or socially oriented. Good leadership balances these tendencies.

Task-oriented leaders tend to emphasize the job or the task to be done, as opposed to individuals or groups. Task-oriented leaders are always tempted to ignore individuals, run roughshod over people, use or manipulate people, fail to maintain group cohesiveness, emphasize formal procedure, and substitute their agenda for group goals—all in their consuming passion to get things done. These serious flaws are not inevitable, but such tendencies often are found in church leaders. Good spiritual leaders may be task oriented, but they carefully avoid the pitfalls associated with task orientation.

Socially-oriented (sometimes referred to as people-oriented) leaders tend to emphasize individuals or groups, as opposed to tasks or jobs. These leaders tend to lack goals (other than the goal of maintaining harmony), spend an exorbitant amount of time on process and procedure, fail to mobilize and motivate people to achieve worthwhile objectives, emphasize informality, overstress unity, and tend to be too sensitive to critics—all in their consuming passion to maintain cohesiveness in the group and pleasantness in interpersonal relationships. Again, some excellent leaders are socially oriented, but avoid succumbing to the temptations of such an orientation.

Excellence in leadership behavior requires both task and people orientation. The best leadership is not a balance between task and social dimensions, as though the leader is partly task oriented and partly socially oriented, or sometimes one and sometimes the other. Rather, the leader must be interested in both dimensions of leadership, never neglecting one for the other.

Every leader has a tendency in one direction or another, and perfect balance is probably impossible to attain, but the best leaders concentrate on both dimensions. A task emphasis may predominate when the group is unmotivated, indifferent, or lackadaisical about achieving goals. A people orientation may predominate when the group is fragmented or when policy-making issues are being addressed. Nevertheless, the best leaders do not favor one orientation at the expense of the other.

Some churches have some leaders who are task oriented, but who are complemented by others who are people oriented. A balance achieved in this way is better than no balance at all, but it is still not as advantageous as the balance displayed by excellent leaders who are both task and people oriented.

The best examples are biblical. Jesus was the perfect leader. He was passionately devoted to getting the job done, and nothing deterred him from the mission committed to him by the Father: "For I have come down from heaven not to do my will but to do the will of him who sent me" (John 6:38). Yet, he was equally passionate about the welfare of individuals and the unity of the body: "Holy Father, protect them by the power of your name—the name you gave me—so that they may be one as we are one" (John 17:11).

Similarly, Paul was so task oriented that he was determined to preach the gospel throughout Asia and then in Rome and Spain: "However, I consider my life worth nothing to me, if only I may finish the race and complete the task the Lord Jesus has given me— the task of testifying to the gospel of God's grace" (Acts 20:24). Yet, Paul was zealous for the unity of the church, and he was devoted to his interpersonal relationships with Timothy, Titus, Silas, Onesiphorus, Lydia, Phoebe, Epaphras, Priscilla and Aquila, and many others. Paul could not be accused of being so interested in task that he ran roughshod over people or was indifferent to people; nor could he be accused of neglecting his major tasks in favor of socially harmonious relationships. Task and people merged in his thinking; it was unthinkable to divorce the two. As Gangel points out, "It is a style which recognizes the inherent value of the individual and the worth of human relations not only as a means to an end, but as an end in itself within the Christian community."[12]

Summary

The numerous problems of leadership style are confusing and complicated. Mistakes are sure to be made; even the best leaders are not infallible. But errors can be minimized if leaders under-

12. Gangel, *Competent to Lead*, 10.

stand the tensions of leadership style and carefully balance their priorities.

The first necessity is to balance two equally clear lines of biblical teaching. Spiritual leaders are to be overseers, not lords, over God's heritage, the church. The church is to obey and submit, but must exercise discernment so as not to be blindly obeisant or servile. Leaders must not abuse their authority, and followers must see that they don't. Christ is the head of the church, and leaders must be careful not to usurp him in their use of authority.

The authority of spiritual leaders is that of the Word of God spoken through them. Obedience accorded to leaders is due to the Word which is proclaimed, not to the persons themselves or to the goals and plans of leaders. The personal preferences of leaders are not to be thrust upon the church.

Some leaders are basically task oriented and others are socially oriented. Excellence in leadership demands emphasis on both jobs to be done and relationships among people. Good spiritual leaders do not see people as mere instruments to accomplish the task or as peripheral to the task; people are of inherent value as ends in themselves.

7

The Struggle of Leadership
Authority

Some of the tough questions about leadership involve the use of influence, power, or authority (words used interchangeably in this context). Leadership involves some form of influence brought to bear upon a group of constituents. What is or is not appropriate use of that power? How much authority or power is appropriate for church leaders and to what extent are church leaders to be held accountable to their constituencies or to external authorities?

Leaders have differed widely in their answers to these questions, depending upon their personal convictions, biblical interpretations, ecclesiastical traditions, and the sensitivity of their consciences. Many have taken a pragmatic approach that rather crassly suggests that a good end justifies virtually any means of achieving it. Some also have assumed that power should be gained to the extent allowed by followers. At the other extreme, there are those who have been so ethically tender that they have been reluctant to use any persuasive efforts; they have eschewed authority and, as a result, their effectiveness is minimal. Effectiveness requires influence, but spiritual leadership is limited by severe biblical constraints.

The Power Game

Is leadership merely manipulation of people to achieve goals? Any thinking person recognizes that the methods used by Adolf Hitler, for example, were base and unscrupulous. But it is a great deal more difficult to discern the proper use of authority by spiritual leaders who desire to move a congregation toward the achievement of a worthwhile goal. Between the clear, agreed-upon extremities of right and wrong there are infinite shades of gray.

Most spiritual leaders emphatically deny that they covet power. Yet, many leaders are self-deceived and compromised in their zeal to accomplish their objectives. It is easy to convince oneself that the achievement of a worthwhile objective justifies a questionable maneuver. One can then become obtuse about the tactic, unaware that the methodology is deceptive or manipulative and that behind the method there is the madness of one who thirsts for power or control.[1]

Self-deception about one's behavior and motives is a potential hazard for all who are in positions of authority. A taste of power whets one's appetite for more of it. Leaders ought never to forget Lord Acton's assertion: "Power tends to corrupt and absolute power corrupts absolutely." The illusion of power also corrupts. For some people, it takes only a moment for the intoxication of power to pollute. The church must always be alert and beware of such people.

There are also church leaders who have no thirst for personal authority or control, those who sincerely desire that good things be accomplished and that God's will be done. It often seems to such leaders that the only way to get things done efficiently is to dominate followers and control decisions. In their righteous zeal, they assume the stance of benevolent dictators, thereby ceasing to be guides and arrogating for themselves an authority that is beyond strict scriptural limits (Matt. 20:25–26; 1 Pet. 5:3).

Dominating behavior in some leaders is often rationalized with

---

1. All spiritual leaders should read *The Power Delusion*, by Anthony Campolo, Jr. (Wheaton: Victor, 1983).

the comment, "It's the only way to get people to *move*." Of course, such an arrogant statement is merely another way of saying, "People are too dumb and recalcitrant to make any good decisions for themselves; after all, what are *sheep*, anyway?" These leaders reveal their extraordinarily low view of humanity. People are not dolts, however; they must be treated with respect by spiritual leaders. Good leaders entrust people with responsibility and guide them in its use, thus enabling them to fulfill their potential. All of this is simply a way of saying that good leaders train leaders; they don't subjugate followers.

The question of leadership authority is a personal one, and there are many differences of opinion. However, regardless of ecclesiastical tradition or personal inclinations, church leaders must not allow themselves to become insensitive to their ways of handling authority and influencing decisions. Some methods are dubious or plainly wrong. A few examples will illustrate.

Distortion

A pastor desperately wanted his church to begin a building program, but most of the members failed to see a need sufficient to justify an increased indebtedness. In his effort to convince the church that the building program was needed, the pastor padded attendance and membership statistics to make it appear the church was growing faster than it was, neglected to remove from the records the names of those who no longer attended, and used both the pulpit and weekly newsletters to declare the church's need for expansion. The pastor's methods of bringing pressure to bear (using authority) were to misrepresent facts and to advance his ideas by using one-way communication, thus avoiding opportunity for debate or presentation of contrary opinions. He also mixed his personal ideas about a building program with his declaration of the Word of God, making it appear that his ideas carried the imprimatur of God. Many leaders are deluded enough to think they possess the mind of God on every issue.

Fear and Threat

A wealthy trustee with fiscally conservative leanings constantly warned the members of a planning committee that an economic depression was coming and the church was already too deeply in debt to consider expansion. He clearly implied that if the church didn't abort its plans to expand, he and his extended family would be forced to find fellowship elsewhere. The church was too small to risk losing such a family and felt forced to yield to his opinion. The tactics used by the trustee were threat and fear of fiscal calamity.

Guilt

In an effort to promote a faltering program, a church leader said, "If you really love God you will be present for this meeting," "You don't want to fail again, do you?" or "All of God's truly faithful people will support this effort with sacrificial giving of time and money." The leader used guilt as his primary motivational strategy. It is often suggested that church leaders use the wedge of guilt more than any other tool to persuade people to action or to get people to cooperate with church programs.

Bribery and Shabby Politics

A church leader involved in the music program wanted a church board to decide to purchase a new church organ. In preparation for the forthcoming vote, the leader systematically invited the members of the board to lunch, shrewdly argued for buying the organ, and picked up the luncheon tab. Members with somewhat less clout were invited for mid-morning coffee. A few very influential board members and their families were invited home for a steak dinner. The leader's efforts centered on ingratiating himself and bribing board members for their votes, with the amount of the bribe defined by the perceived power of the member. He expected that people would feel indebted to him, thus giving him their votes when the time came. Some people may deny that these power tactics are shabby politics and bribery, but at the very least the methodology is questionable.

These methods of using power may be effective in accomplishing the leader's will, but they are unethical to most sensitive leaders. Other abuses of authority or attempts to influence are not so obvious. The spiritual leader must develop a sensitivity to the methods he uses to persuade. Honesty with oneself is always difficult, but it is indispensable to spiritual leadership in the use of authority.

Appropriate Leadership Power

Leadership, in part, is power, authority, or influence. Only one kind of power is moral in a spiritual setting:

> We may speak of Christian authority as the power to influence opinion, induce belief, and so lead to action in areas defined as spiritual by a group of persons who acknowledge Christ as Lord. The power is considered legitimate when it conveys the spirit of Christ to others. It is to be exercised in the spirit of humble service which Jesus exemplified with his disciples.[2]

The basis of true power in church leadership is the power of personal spiritual authenticity. Spiritual authenticity is the validity of the Word of God and the Spirit of God demonstrated in the lives of leaders. People who lack such authenticity should not be entrusted with authority or official positions in the church. The power of spiritual leadership does not center in artifice, but in the leader's validation of scriptural truth. The leader influences others not by the power of personality or by persuasive tricks, but by a life irradiated and empowered by the Holy Spirit. Such a life forms the foundation of any spiritual leader's ethical behavior.

Spiritual authenticity has everything to do with the quality of the leader's ministry and the kind of influence used. Church leaders should not be selected and entrusted with authority merely because of their expertise or skills as evaluated by secular standards, and yet this is often done. Trustees, for example, are frequently nominated and elected because of obvious knowledge about financial matters, even though they may not demonstrate spiritual maturity.

Ministerial service and spiritual authenticity must be the basic criteria for leadership, as Dietrich Bonhoeffer stressed in his extraordinary summary statement on authority:

> Jesus made authority in the fellowship dependent upon brotherly service. Genuine spiritual authority is to be found only where the ministry of hearing, helping, bearing, and proclaiming is carried out. Every cult of personality that emphasizes the distinguished qualities, virtues, and talents of another person, even although these

2. Samuel Southard, *Pastoral Authority in Personal Relationships* (Nashville: Abingdon, 1969), 29.

be of an altogether spiritual nature, is worldly and has no place in the Christian community. . . . The bishop is the simple, faithful man, sound in faith and life, who rightly discharges his duties to the Church. His authority lies in the exercise of his ministry. In the man himself there is nothing to admire.[3]

Any leadership in the church not grounded upon this solid foundation is wrongly based and must be rejected. Of course, additional qualifications are necessary for many specific responsibilities.

What then is leadership authority? What does the church leader do to influence or to exercise authority in a manner compatible with spiritual authenticity? Spiritual authority, based upon spiritual authenticity, is demonstrated in the following ways.

Modeling Christian Discipleship

Ethical leaders influence people by modeling true Christian discipleship. True leaders think and take action with a conscious desire "to make [themselves] a model for you to follow" (2 Thess. 3:9). This kind of leadership is powerful, but never manipulative. Good leaders work hard, and others are then stimulated to work hard. Good leaders do not merely tell others to give sacrificially; good leaders themselves give sacrificially. Good leaders do not merely conduct classes on how to witness; rather, they take people with them when they witness.[4] The main motivation of leaders in doing many good things is not to get others to imitate them. They do acts of ministry because they are scripturally mandated. The side benefit is that others follow their example.

No one has ever been so authoritative as Jesus Christ, not only because he was God incarnate on earth, but because people recognized that his words were authenticated in his life. There was a radical and obvious difference in him personally, in his value systems and lifestyle, and this difference distinguished him from all other teachers of the law.

Similarly, the apostle Paul modeled discipleship, and his modeling was his most powerful way to influence his converts:

Even though you have ten thousand guardians in Christ, you do not have many fathers, for in Christ Jesus I became your father

---

3. Dietrich Bonhoeffer, *Life Together* (New York: Macmillan, 1954), 108.
4. The basic premise of the Evangelism Explosion methodology.

> through the gospel. Therefore I urge you to imitate me. For this reason I am sending to you Timothy. . . . He will remind you of my way of life in Christ Jesus, which agrees with what I teach everywhere in every church. [1 Cor. 4:15–17]

True spiritual power does not lie in self-assertion, but in the example of a worthy parent's self-denial. A good father does not raise the question, "Who is master of the house?" Nevertheless, his authority is effective because of his commitment to care for his family and his worthy example of devotion. Charles Spurgeon was correct when he preached: "I am persuaded that the greatest power we can get over our fellow men is the power which comes of consecration and holiness."[5]

Leaders who are dearly loved for their virtuous, caring, sacrificial lifestyle will be followed. Such leaders are influential; they gain a following not because of clever methodologies, but because of evident spiritual authenticity in the stresses and strains of daily life. They do not merely preach; they practice, and the practice gives credence to their message and power to their leadership.

Teaching Scriptural Truth

Spiritual leaders use power ethically in their teaching. Some of the most powerful people in history have been teachers. A good teacher facilitates the achievement of human potential, molds ideas and life principles, and shapes people's lives. Others may dominate and force submission, but their power is usually temporary and superficial. An excellent teacher fashions better people and, ultimately, a different society. Again, our most prominent example is Jesus. "When Jesus finished saying these things [the Sermon on the Mount], the crowds were amazed at his teaching, because he taught as one who had authority, and not as their teachers of the law" (Matt. 7:28–29). Jesus took twelve men and, during a short ministry, he poured his life into them, taught them with words supported by example, and radically changed eleven of them to alter the world. The best of spiritual leaders conceive their task to be that of teaching. Barnabas took Paul and encouraged him in the ministry. Later, Paul took Silas, Timothy, and many others, and discipled them.

5. Charles Spurgeon, *All-Round Ministry* (reprint ed.; Carlisle, Penn.: Banner of Truth, 1972), 245.

Spiritual leaders are teachers whose teaching is validated by their lifestyle. The overseer must be "able to teach" (1 Tim. 3:2). Paul counseled Timothy, "Command and teach these things . . . [and] the things you have heard me say in the presence of many witnesses entrust to reliable men who will also be qualfied to teach others" (1 Tim. 4:11; 2 Tim. 2:2).

Such teaching is central to the biblical description of leaders as rulers. Leadership's function is associated in Scripture with authoritative communication of God's Word: "Remember your leaders (Greek *hegēomai*) who spoke the word of God to you" (Heb. 13:7). Jay Adams defines ruling as

> bringing sheep *together* as a flock, or congregation, teaching and helping them to live, learn, love, and labor together for Jesus Christ. . . . [Ruling is] the authoritative instruction in and application of the Word of God to the individual and corporate activities of the sheep.[6]

John R. W. Stott similarly emphasizes this authority of spiritual leadership: "Here, then, is the preacher's authority. It depends on the closeness of his adherence to the text he is handling, that is, on the accuracy with which he has understood it and on the forcefulness with which it has spoken to his own soul."[7] This description of discipleship ministry is much different from defining the spiritual ruler as one who gives orders to the church or as one who makes decisions for the church to carry out.

The true power of the spiritual teacher does not lie in personal ability or worldly wisdom, but, as Paul taught, "a demonstration of the Spirit's power" (1 Cor. 2:4). Spiritual leaders use their power ethically when they are preparing "God's people for works of service, so that the body of Christ may be built up" (Eph. 4:12) and "admonishing and teaching everyone with all wisdom, so that we may present everyone perfect in Christ" (Col. 1:28).

Of course, some church leaders may not be particularly gifted in formal teaching. They may use their abilities in ministries not directly related to teaching and in ways compatible with their talents. This does not change the truth that true spiritual leaders, especially pastors and elders, ethically lead by teaching, persuading with facts, sound logic, reasoning, and sincerity.

6. Jay Adams, *Shepherding God's Flock* (Grand Rapids: Baker, 1980), 325.
7. John R. W. Stott, *The Preacher's Portrait* (Grand Rapids: Eerdmans, 1961), 30.

Guiding to Maturity

Spiritual leaders are spiritually-sighted people who are guides, who know and point out the way because they themselves have traveled on that way. Jesus severely criticized the Pharisees of his day: "Woe to you, blind guides! . . . You strain out a gnat but swallow a camel" (Matt. 23:16, 24).

Guides assist people to reach a destination which they would not be apt to reach on their own. Guides supply advice, counsel, and companionship in practical and spiritual affairs. This is the meaning of shepherding, caring for all kinds of people and for the church as a body.

The power of ecclesiastical leaders is dependent upon acquired respect and demonstrated expertise in loving service. This authority of spiritual leaders "arises out of the concrete incarnation of the spirit of loving service which by God's help becomes present in the care of souls [guidance]."[8]

The essence of leadership ministry lies in deep person-to-person relationships in which leaders recommend, advise, and counsel the church and its members in spiritual matters. Bonhoeffer stresses this profound truth:

> Genuine authority knows that it is bound in the strictest sense by the saying of Jesus: "One is your Master, even Christ; and all ye are brethren" (Matthew 23:8). The Church does not need brilliant personalities but faithful servants of Jesus and the brethren. Not in the former but in the latter is the lack. The Church will place its confidence only in the simple servant of the Word of Jesus Christ because it knows that then it will be *guided,* not according to human wisdom and human conceit, but by the Word of the Good Shepherd [emphasis added].[9]

A guide does not command or manipulate. Rather, a guide points the way toward spiritual maturity and gives sound reasons why a specific direction should be considered. A worthy guide is not one who thinks for other people, but one who assists people to think for themselves. Authoritative guidance works for people's maturity, not for their dependency. An excellent guide does not

8. Daniel Williams, *The Minister and the Care of Souls* (New York: Harper and Row, 1961), 43.
9. Bonhoeffer, *Life Together*, 109.

merely point people in the right direction; rather, the guide assists people to become competent in determining their own direction. The worthy guide does not tell the wilderness traveler which way the compass points; he shows the traveler how to read the compass and the maps.

Church history is replete with examples of evil guides, those who used various tactics to gain control over followers, often for selfish advantage. Unworthy guides do not want people to become independent thinkers; rather, they want people's deference and dependency.

Followers themselves must take responsibility to recognize those false guides who motivate by playing upon people's capacity to hate, latent fears, penchant for hero figures, or guilt feelings. Corrupt, fraudulent, and unscrupulous leaders are successful in attaining an unjust power only when followers cooperate in their own victimization. James Jones, relying on illicit tactics, led 930 people to death in Guyana, but the people who died allowed themselves to be manipulated. Submission to spiritual leadership is biblically commanded, but followers are also expected to be spiritually discerning enough to recognize and reject false prophets and all those who desire self-aggrandizement. Therefore, leaders of immature people are at the greatest risk of abusing their leadership prerogatives, because their followers' lack of experience diminishes their spiritual discernment.

Spiritual guides do not strive for power, except for the power that is released in their followers. Worthy leaders constantly think in terms of removing impediments to individual development, enhancing the power of constituents. Unworthy authority figures consciously or unconsciously think in terms of maintaining and enhancing their own power, creating blind trust in themselves as leaders. Unethical leaders want followers to trust their judgment without questioning and defer to their plans without debate. Worthy spiritual guides believe in the potential of their followers, create a climate in which followers mature, encourage the free exchange of ideas, and cultivate the followers' participation in decision making.

The Authority of Clergy

A special word must be said about the authority of clergy, but to do so is to inevitably trigger dissent because of the dissimilarity in church traditions. Agreement across denominational lines is impossible, and the scriptural evidence is far from conclusive.

Some scholars suggest that the rite of ordination invests an individual with a status and an authority distinct from those of all other church leaders. John Calvin believed that there are four orders within a hierarchal church structure: pastor, teacher, elder, and deacon. Teachers, elders, and deacons are below pastors in both authority and status, primarily because pastors are ordained and others are not.

Episcopal and Catholic traditions invest clergy with jurisdictional powers over the church. Ordained leaders (priests) are invested with the authority to administer the sacraments and make most church decisions, although they are accountable to a bishop.

Congregational church government sees little or no invested authority in the professional clergy which is not shared with other spiritual, nonprofessional leaders, although some exponents of congregationalism would grant the authority to administer the ordinances only to those properly ordained by the church.

It seems apparent that ordination was never intended to mark professional ministers as a separate caste within the Christian community. Rather, ordination originally was a way for the church to recognize and publicly confirm the special gifts and calling of individuals in preaching, teaching, or certain other specialized ministries. Hence, ordination was not instituted to grant decision-making authority over the church body, but to commission individuals to exercise special gifts in clearly defined ways, especially in preaching and teaching. H. Richard Niebuhr and Daniel D. Williams describe how clergy gradually assumed greater and greater authority in ecclesiastical tradition.[10]

Whatever one's ecclesiastical persuasion, it should be agreed that authority rests ultimately with the head of the body, Christ, and that all spiritual leaders are accountable to him. Clergy are not to run the church as authority figures, but they are themselves under the authority of Christ. Therefore, they are undershepherds.

In addition, many traditions believe that clergy, like other leaders, are accountable to the church itself as well as to Christ. The church, in most cases, has authority to retain or remove clergy, as

10. H. Richard Niebuhr and Daniel D. Williams, eds., *The Ministry in Historical Perspective* (New York: Harper and Brothers, 1956).

well as authority to ordain and defrock. Hence, the church itself possesses an authority greater than that of its leaders, including clergy. Those who differ from this opinion suggest that the authority of Christ is mediated through leadership, particularly through clergy, and that the church must respect the will of the clergy as the will of Christ himself. Some leaders believe they are accountable to no one except God.

It seems presumptuous, however, for clergy to advance the notion that they alone have insight concerning the will of Christ for the church. It seems more reasonable to suggest that the church should retain certain decision-making authority under the headship of Christ. The New Testament churches chose leaders (Acts 6:3, 5; 14:23), commissioned missionaries (Acts 13:2–3), exercised discipline (Matt. 18:15–17; 1 Cor. 5:4–5, 13; 2 Thess. 3:6, 14–15), and seemed to reserve certain other rights for the body as a whole. The church certainly participated in major decisions (see Acts 15).[11]

For the sake of conducting business decently and in order, New Testament churches delegated authority to their leaders (or simply expected them) to administer their daily activities. However, some modern circumstances differ dramatically from those in New Testament times. It seems wise for the church to retain authority to approve doctrinal positions and by-laws, incur sizable indebtedness, purchase or sell property, receive or excommunicate members, adopt budgets, receive reports, act on major recommendations, and select or remove its primary spiritual leaders, including professional staff. Beyond these things, and perhaps a few others, it seems prudent for congregations to invest their leaders with authority to act on their behalf. Leaders, including clergy, who consistently abuse their invested authority should be removed from their positions of responsibility. Unethical behavior of leaders cannot be tolerated by the church.

Every clergy person should soberly reflect upon the words of Anthony Campolo, Jr.:

> Few people know the rhetoric of servanthood better than the clergy. And yet so many of them, even unconsciously, are on power trips. It may be that some were attracted to the ministry because they saw in the role of the minister the opportunity to exercise power. Clergymen of this type have learned to play their power games with a

11. See chapter 12 for an interpretation of the decision-making process in Acts 15.

cleverness that keep most people from ever suspecting what they are really about.[12]

Clergy should have some spiritually mature people to whom they are accountable. Such people have a sacred responsibility to see that its pastors do not usurp authority or exceed biblical constraints. Jesus used harsh words to describe religious leaders who gloried in their power, lording it over others: "Woe to you Pharisees, because you love the most important seats in the synagogues and greetings in the marketplaces" (Luke 11:43).

Submission to Authority

When leaders have the proper spiritual qualifications and conduct themselves as models, teachers, and guides within carefully-defined parameters, the church is required to respect them and follow their leadership. Rebellion against such leadership is not only unethical, but also rejection of God's appointed order for the church. Authority in the church—if it is legitimately exercised—is Christ's authority.

What does submission to leadership authority mean in practical terms? Submission does not mean that every recommendation or every teaching of leaders must be adopted or believed, for human leaders are never infallible, and followers must be discerning enough to reject bad counsel. However, spiritual guidance offered by ethically behaving leaders must never be rejected lightly or for personal reasons, and rejection of it must be justified by the most stringent, honest, cogent argument.

Further, any rejection of the spiritual counsel of the church's leaders must be done in a way that is respectful of God's order in the church. Adams wisely states this sobering truth:

> Every member within the flock must grant to the leadership all proper deference and great respect, but at the same time Christ has made each member responsible to exercise individual judgment concerning the leadership that he follows. . . . Yet, if a member disagrees with the decisions of the leadership, and because of conscience before God finds that he must refuse to submit to the orders that they give, he must do even that submissively (i.e., in a proper

12. Campolo, *The Power Delusion*, 42.

spirit that acknowledges the position and authority that Christ has granted to the leaders of His Church). Moreover, he must recognize the grave danger in which he may be placing himself by such a refusal. It is possible otherwise that:

1) He may be found to be opposing Christ Himself.

2) He may be showing disrespect for Christ, by disregarding the authority that He invested in His officers. Because of these dangers, only after great care and willingness to be taught and corrected by the leadership as they explain the Word of God to him, may he refuse to submit to them.[13]

Some of Adams's expressions are objectionable (e.g., "the orders that they give"), but the essence of his argument is certainly valid.

Many congregations are traumatized, crippled, and divided because members have not understood that such submission is required by God. Members may not refuse to submit to spiritual leadership for any reason except that they are convinced that their leaders have failed to base their guidance upon the Word of God, failed to properly discern God's direction for the church, and failed to demonstrate the spirit of humble service to Christ.

Of course, the rub comes when church leaders make decisions, propose recommendations, or carry out action on matters in which there are no specific scriptural guidelines. Must church members submit to leaders' decisions, adopt their recommendations, and agree with such actions? There is room for difference of opinion here, but it seems reasonable to propose that members may disagree respectfully with the wisdom of their leaders in these matters, may request changes, and in certain extreme cases, may find it necessary to overrule their leaders or remove them from their positions. However, such actions cannot be carried out with a capricious, cavalier, disrespectful attitude toward leaders.

On the other hand, leaders must be extremely careful in taking action that cannot be supported biblically or that is not specifically delegated to them by the church. They must scrutinize their own motives to be sure that they are not acting selfishly or imprudently. They must scrupulously observe the biblical mandates about discernment, wisdom, prudence, and concern for the spiritual health of the church.

Leaders must be particularly careful that they are not merely

13. Adams, *Shepherding God's Flock*, 330.

attempting to inflict their personal preferences on the congregation. Some church leaders become pathologically willful. Leaders must be of sufficient integrity and honesty to be sure that the issue does not become a power struggle between personalities or positions. Leaders must not reduce leadership to a competitive sport in which they must win and in which their opinion must prevail. As Andre Bustanoby has correctly said, "Power struggles between autocratic people have divided many a church into warring camps. Too often it is not the issues that are responsible for factionalism; the real problem is with the autocratic personalities who lead the power struggle."[14]

In other words, there are times when leaders take action that flows not from a serious, spiritual concern for the welfare of the church and a prayerful discernment of God's will, but from their own authoritarian personalities and desire for control. This kind of behavior often provokes a spirit of rebellion or hostility in the congregation, and it becomes impossible to maintain proper respect and deference.

Many difficulties and misunderstandings in the relationship between leaders and church members could be avoided if churches would clearly delineate what authority its leaders may and may not exercise. Some churches (especially those with loosely structured congregational traditions) have internal power struggles and interpersonal strife because the parameters of authority are not clearly defined in the church by-laws and understood by all. It is a rare church that has a well-written document that carefully spells out the lines and the limits of authority. Poor organizational documents invite abuse of authority.

Leaders of the church frequently make decisions that the congregation never empowered (or never thought it empowered) them to make. At other times, leaders are frustrated by too-stringent controls placed upon them by their congregations so that they do not have liberty to take any reasonable action.

The important thing is that there must be no jealousy between the congregation and its leaders. Churches that refuse their leaders the authority to make reasonable decisions merely pay lip service to leadership; they deny leaders the right to lead; and, more seri-

14. Andre Bustanoby, *You Can Change Your Personality: Make It a Spiritual Asset* (Grand Rapids: Zondervan, 1976), 74.

ously, they refuse God's order for the church. For their part, leaders must guard against a thirst for power and control; they must not claim divine sanction for their personal opinions.

Balance in this matter is crucial. Imbalance in favor of empowering leadership with too much authority risks denial of the headship of Christ, weakens necessary congregational authority, makes leadership training difficult, and encourages domination by leaders. Imbalance in favor of congregational authority frustrates the appropriate function of leadership and cripples the church's ministry.

The church is a theocracy, not a democracy. Christ has deemed it necessary for church affairs to be administered by spiritual overseers who preside and guide, but who do not dictate. Leaders are themselves under authority and held accountable to Christ and, to some extent, to the church. Only when this delicate balance is maintained can there be both ethical leaders and ethical followers.

Summary

Spiritual leaders are meant to influence opinion, induce belief, and lead people to action—and to do so ethically. The proper authority of spiritual leaders lies in their spiritual authenticity, the validity of the Word of God, and the ministry of God's Spirit demonstrated in their lives. Good spiritual leaders have enormous ethical power as models, instructors, and guides when they behave according to biblical guidelines. No one should seek an authority beyond these things.

It is questionable whether clergy have any special authority besides that shared with other spiritual leaders in the church. Their real power lies in their proclamation of divine truth and in the power conferred upon them by the esteem and affection of the church as a result of their personal example and competence as servants. In the beginning ordination was intended not to confer jurisdictional control over the church, but to recognize the privileges of ministry. In most ecclesiastical traditions, the church retains significant authority under the headship of Christ. Clergy should be accountable to some spiritually mature people and to the church itself.

Church members are required to respect and submit to spiritual leaders who properly conduct themselves under scriptural constraints and church by-laws. Rebellion against spiritual leaders is rejection of God's appointed order for the church. This does not mean that every recommendation or instruction of leaders must be adopted or believed, for human leaders are never infallible. Church members must be spiritually discerning enough to reject poor counsel, but differences of personal opinion or personality clashes are not acceptable grounds for rejecting leaders' guidance.

Balance in this matter is crucial. Imbalance that gives excessive power to leaders risks denial of the headship of Christ, weakens appropriate congregational authority, and encourages autocratic leaders. For their part, leaders must always remember that they are under authority. Imbalance in favor of democracy frustrates Christ's order for the church and cripples the church's ministry. Only when this delicate balance is maintained can leaders ethically use their authority and followers properly submit to that authority.

8

The Test of Leadership
Effectiveness

Whatis true of parents is also true of Christian leaders: some are obvious successes and others are conspicuous failures. Good parents sometimes are burdened with rebellious and wayward children; some apparently poor parents are blessed with outstanding children. It seems that the sovereign grace of God blesses some leaders despite what they do. Other leaders seem to do everything right, and yet there is little perceived success. The reasons are not always readily discernible.

Effectiveness in Spiritual Leadership

By worldly standards, leaders are judged to be successful or effective when their goals are achieved through their followers. The businessman whose financial report shows significant profit, the corporate executive whose subordinates perform their tasks well, the politician whose proposals are enacted into law—all are judged to be successful.

By contrast, spiritual leaders cannot be judged by any of these materialistic criteria, although this is often done. The number of people in church, the size of the annual budget, the impressiveness of church structures, the involvement of members in church activities, and the multiplicity of programs are frequently the criteria by which the effectiveness of church leaders is evaluated. The church can be a beehive of activity, erect magnificent buildings, and be packed with people, yet be ineffective in any meaningful ministry.

Church leaders often are judged to be successes if the external indications of physical growth are impressive. Pastors frequently move to larger ministries because of their reputations as producers of dazzling statistics. Those who become popular on the speaking circuit frequently preside over statistically successful ministries. There are compelling temptations and pressures for leaders to produce physical and temporal results. This is tragic, but human nature makes such things inevitable, unless there is consistent effort to avoid the materialistic success syndrome.[1]

Most management books say that goals should be quantitative and measurable, but spiritual goals do not always lend themselves to such standards. Effectiveness in ministry should be evaluated according to spiritual standards that are difficult, perhaps impossible, to quantify. Spiritual leaders should consider these criteria of effectiveness in ministry:

> We measure the effectiveness of the leader not in terms of the leadership he *exercises*, but in terms of the leadership he *evokes*; not in terms of power over others, but in terms of the power he releases in others; not in terms of the goals he sets up and the directions he gives, but in terms of the goals and plans of action persons work out for themselves with his help; not in terms alone of products and projects completed, but in terms of growth in competence, sense of responsibility, and personal satisfactions among many participants. Under this kind of leadership it is not always clear at any given moment just who is leading, nor is this very important.[2]

---

1. All spiritual leaders would profit from reading Kent Hughes and Barbara Hughes, *Liberating Ministry from the Success Syndrome* (Wheaton: Tyndale House, 1987).

2. Grace Elliott, *How to Help Groups Make Decisions* (New York: Association, 1959), 43.

Leaders must constantly keep in mind the basic task of spiritual leadership: developing relationships with people in such a way that they are enabled to formulate and achieve biblical goals for groups and individuals that meet real needs. In achieving this objective, individuals and the church body grow to spiritual maturity and reach out to the community and to the world. Leaders accomplish the critical task of leadership by serving people so that they are motivated, inspired, and enabled to accomplish their fullest potential. Leadership's primary goal is that people

> will no longer be infants, tossed back and forth by the waves, and blown here and there by every wind of teaching and by the cunning and craftiness of men in their deceitful scheming. Instead, speaking the truth in love, we will in all things grow up into him who is the Head, that is, Christ. From him the whole body, joined and held together by every supporting ligament, grows and builds itself up in love, as each part does its work. [Eph. 4:14–16]

In an effort to delineate leadership effectiveness in Christian ministry, the following criteria are suggested. Other things certainly could be added to the list, but these are central to effectiveness in spiritual ministry.

Clarity in Philosophy of Ministry

Excellence in spiritual leadership is judged by the clarity of the group's philosophy of ministry that is formed and enacted with the leader's help, and often through the leader's initiatives. A body of believers that knows where it is going and how to get there is a church that has effective leadership. Churches with poor leadership drift along without understanding their purpose, objectives, strategies, and place in their communities.

The expression *philosophy of ministry* is comparatively new, but good church leaders had a clear philosophy of ministry long before the term came into use. The apostle Paul, for example, had a distinct philosophy of ministry. A few of Paul's philosophical tenets are these:

1. Paul emphasized that the gospel is the power of God for the salvation of everyone who believes, first for the Jew, then for the Gentile (Rom. 1:16).

2. Paul endeavored to preach the gospel where Christ was not known. He did not want to build on someone else's foundation (Rom. 15:20).
3. Paul did not preach with "wise and persuasive words, but with a demonstration of the Spirit's power" (1 Cor. 2:4).
4. Paul taught publicly and from house to house (Acts 20:20).
5. Paul worked with his own hands; he paid his own way in order to make himself a model for people to follow (2 Thess. 3:7–9).

All spiritual leaders who are worthy of their positions help their constituency to clarify and articulate basic principles of their ministry. The ingredients of this philosophy inevitably vary from church to church. No single ideology fits every church and perhaps no two are ever identical. The concepts may be outlined in broad strokes or carefully detailed, but they are always clear, unmistakable, explicated, and understood by the church constituency. It is not sufficient to have a fuzzy conception of what the church is all about.

A basic philosophy of ministry must include answers to questions about the church's mission, its strategies for accomplishing its mission, the methodologies it will use, and its distinct, unique place in its community. Of course, there are other pertinent questions as well. The specific answers to these questions may vary according to the church size, available resources, the community, the culture, and other things. Yet, without clear direction, the organization or institution will merely drift, doing many good things perhaps, but without reason, purpose, or guidance. Frank Tillapaugh is correct: "Before a church spends much time on methodology it should spend a lot of time on philosophy of ministry."[3] A good philosophy of ministry, however, includes methodology in addition to ideological principles.

Effective, ministering churches have leaders

1. who can be believed and trusted,
2. who put the interests of the group before personal interests,
3. who help the group define where it is going,
4. who know how to get there or who help the group find out how to get there,

3. Frank Tillapaugh, *The Church Unleashed* (Ventura, Calif.: Regal, 1982), 138.

5. who make the mission seem important, possible, and exciting to the constituency, and

6. who help the constituency to plan a strategy so that realistic goals are achieved.

Sometimes all of this is loosely referred to as vision and direction. Followers are led to feel the mission of the church is vital, their role in the mission is integral, and they are capable of performing their role. All of this is inherent in a philosophy that effectively governs leaders and constituents in all that they do as they serve Christ in the community. In a study of churches, Donald P. Smith found that effective, ministering congregations shared several characteristics, which he dramatized in his report:

> The sense of congregational identity in ministering congregations is striking. They know who they are and what they stand for, and they often feel they are unique. . . . "This is who we are," they will say. "This is what we stand for. . . ." The doors of these congregations are truly open to all who wish to share their vision, but they are not prepared to compromise that vision in order to attract more members. They know who they are, where they are going, and why.[4]

What often separates effectively ministering churches from those that merely maintain a status quo is leaders who instill a sense of identity and direction. Eugene Jennings recognized this dedication to mission in effective leaders: "Great changes in the history of an organization or society generally result from the innovative efforts of a few superior individuals. . . . [T]hey may be possessed by a sense of mission to which they dedicate their total selves."[5]

It is that clear sense of mission, or philosophy of ministry and understanding of identity, by which effective leaders are judged superior in their ability. Effectiveness must be evaluated by this indispensable standard.

A Passion for Evangelism

Evangelism is a significant part of every worthwhile philosophy of ministry. A passion for evangelism—as the apostle Paul had—is contagious and indicates effective spiritual leadership. Good leaders are never content with the status quo or with a maintenance

4. Donald P. Smith, "Shared Ministry," *Theology Today* 36 (October 1979): 338.
5. Eugene Jennings, *An Anatomy of Leadership* (New York: McGraw-Hill, 1972), 1.

ministry. They constantly think of promoting, stimulating, and modeling evangelism to produce real growth in the body. Ineffective leaders may think of growth, but not in evangelistic terms.

Effective church leaders see themselves as preachers and the work of the church as preaching, not in the sense of what professional clergy do in the pulpit on Sunday, but in the sense of biblically heralding (Greek *prokērussō*) the gospel message—the responsibility of all Christians. True spiritual leaders see themselves as ambassadors of Christ: "And he has committed to us the message of reconciliation. We are therefore Christ's ambassadors, as though God were making his appeal through us" (2 Cor. 5:19–20). Leaders infect others with an ambassador's spirit and enthusiasm.

Leaders' effectiveness is determined by whether they are out front in this crucial ministry and by whether they stimulate and inspire others to join their efforts. Poor leaders are content to run programs that have no realistic outreach to the community. A church with no vision for the community and the world is a poor church indeed and far from the biblical standard of excellence.

Growing, effective churches have a passion for evangelism, and behind that passion are leaders whose contagious spirit for outreach has influenced others. Spiritual leaders grasp this essential nature of Christian ministry, and they do not rest until others share their passion.

A Healthy Body of Believers

Effective leaders inevitably and eventually produce a healthy church body. A healthy church is measured not in terms of its size or the number of its programs, but in terms of its unity and its members who are equipped and functioning in the work of the ministry. An unhealthy church is fragmented, or its members are largely spectators watching professionals perform in church services. Poor leaders permit and sometimes unwittingly promote a sit-and-soak and build-the-fortress mentality. Good leaders foster a we're-out-there-doing-it mentality. The healthy church is prepared and stimulated to minister in neighborhoods and communities. "The service begins when the meeting ends," as one deacon put it. A leader is judged effective when the church catches and exercises such a vision.

Effective leaders are impatient with merely maintaining bureaucracy; they have an ability to cut through housekeeping matters and stimulate real ministry. Excellent leaders do not settle for smoothly operating organizational machinery, which often seems sufficient to uninspired congregations.

The production of a functioning body means several things. First, it means that leaders take seriously their responsibility of equipping God's people for the work of the ministry (Eph. 4:12). Effective leaders take a hard look at what the church is doing in its preaching ministry, the Sunday school, small-group Bible studies, women's and men's groups, youth meetings, and senior citizens' meetings. All of these meetings are scrutinized and evaluated by good leaders to determine if they are meeting real needs and preparing people for ministry. At this point leadership has often proved itself inadequate, and also at this point effective leaders are distinguished from mediocre leaders.

The average Christian leader tends to settle for meetings that promote social ends (the warm fuzzies) and/or that dispense biblical information. Social pleasantries are to an extent necessary, but socializing should not be confused with the scriptural concept of spiritual fellowship. Teaching scriptural meaning is good and necessary but must not be confused with discipleship ministry.

Practically every church has people who are theologically astute, but who do not demonstrate a biblical standard of conduct or spiritual maturity. "If dumping content on people produced mature Christians, the church in the United States would be by far the most mature church which history has ever seen."[6] There is little evidence to suggest that people who experience warm fuzzies and who know many theological facts are able to resist temptation, are capable of bearing witness, excel as godly parents or marriage partners, or become mature, functioning Christians.

It is not uncommon to find people in our churches who have been in church meetings and Bible classes since childhood, but at the age of forty or fifty they still have no idea what their spiritual gifts are, how to teach an evangelistic Bible study, how to comfort a grief-stricken person, or how to perform any real ministry. The extent of their involvement has been to sit on a church board or committee, to oil the bureaucratic machinery of the church. Such an observation may seem harsh, but it is accurate.

6. Tillapaugh, *The Church Unleashed*, 134.

Effective leaders do not tolerate this state of affairs. They are willing to initiate programs that will contribute to the task of producing gifted, mature, ministering saints and to eliminate or change nonproductive programs. In other words, as Grace Elliott suggested, effective leaders are not content with exercising leadership; they think constantly about evoking leadership in others. Effective leaders are midwives to ministry because they see to it that Christians are discipled and equipped to fulfill their purpose in the world, according to God's plan. Church structures, programs, and meetings should aim to accomplish this biblical purpose.

There is a temptation for leaders to do things that others should be doing. Leaders who fall into this snare unwittingly cause the church to become functionally crippled. In the divine plan, leaders serve people by training them to function effectively in ministries of their own, not by making them dependent upon the leaders and their abilities. If parishioners develop a way of thinking that shifts the burden of ministry away from themselves and onto the shoulders of a few professionals, leadership has failed. Churches with effective leadership do not have a few superstars who carry the load.

Second, the production of a healthy, functioning body means that leaders administer efficiently the daily affairs of the church. Leaders are to "direct the affairs of the church" (1 Tim. 5:17), but they should not become so bogged down with administrative detail that other crucial ministries are neglected. Nevertheless, administration is vital to a healthy body of believers. Senior pastors deceive themselves if they say, "My real gift is administration and, therefore, I spend 70 percent of my time doing that." If they understood the true nature of pastoral ministry, they would not spend so much time in administration; if they were gifted in it, they wouldn't have to. They would delegate many administrative tasks so that they could major in tasks more fundamental to the pastoral role.

Some leaders may be particularly gifted in administration and therefore work primarily in this area of ministry.[7] It is this administrative ability that Scripture identifies as the gift of "helps." Paul writes, "If a man's gift . . . is leadership, let him govern dili-

---

7. It is questionable whether such leaders should be called pastors. The nature of a pastoral role demands time for prayer, study, preaching-teaching, discipling, and shepherding.

gently" (Rom. 12:8). Paul also speaks of "gifts of administration" (1 Cor. 12:28). This Greek word (*kubernēsis*) "can only [refer] to the specific gifts which qualify a Christian to be a helmsman to his congregation, [that is], a true director of its order and therewith of its life. . . . No society can exist without some order and direction. It is the grace of God to give gifts which equip for government."[8] However, it is a poverty-stricken church that has gifted administrators but is devoid of leaders capable of praying, preaching-teaching, and shepherding. Rather, the New Testament suggests that the true biblical leader does what is necessary in administration, delegates many tasks to others, and prays, studies, preaches, teaches, disciples, and cares for individual needs.

There is confusion and disagreement about the management function of spiritual leaders. Some say flatly, "The responsibility of leaders is not to manage the church."[9] Others believe that leaders possess dictatorial power in the administration of the church.

Despite opinions to the contrary, Scripture plainly assigns some management duties to overseers. The overseer must "manage his own family well" because "if anyone does not know how to manage his own family, how can he take care of God's church?" (1 Tim. 3:4–5).

This book is not about management, but church leaders cannot be effective for long unless they know how to efficiently organize, write, communicate, and administer the policies and programs of the church. But leadership is not merely management. True spiritual leadership extends far beyond the things that tend to be routine, but if these things are not done efficiently, there is little time left for the more important functions of church leadership.

Great care must be exercised in management functions so that these tasks are not performed in a domineering, overbearing fashion. John R. W. Stott warns against this: "To set ourselves up, therefore, as the fathers, masters and teachers of men, is to usurp the glory of the Eternal Trinity, and to arrogate to ourselves an authority over men which belongs to God alone."[10] It is this kind

8. Gerhard Kittel, ed., *Theological Dictionary of the New Testament* (Grand Rapids: Eerdmans, 1964), "kubernesis."

9. Larry Richards and Clyde Hoeldtke, *A Theology of Church Leadership* (Grand Rapids: Zondervan, 1980), 92.

10. John R. W. Stott, *The Preacher's Portrait* (Grand Rapids: Eerdmans, 1961), 83. See Stott's entire chapter on the leader as spiritual father for an excellent exposition of this subject.

of domineering authority to which Jesus objected when he said: "Call no man your father on earth, for you have one Father, who is in heaven" (Matt. 23:9 RSV).

The management style of church leaders should be that of a spiritual father's relationship of understanding, affection, gentleness, compassion, and nurture with his children. Any management on the part of leaders is unscriptural if it fails to communicate these basic attitudes.

Scripture teaches that leaders do have an important management function in the church, but it is management carried out through a philosophy and methodology very different from that found anywhere except in the finest of Christian homes. Myron Rush emphasized this: "It is tragic that so many Christian organizations have accepted the world's philosophy of management. They are attempting to accomplish God's work using a management philosophy diametrically opposed to biblical principles."[11]

Jay Adams stated the same truth:

> Insofar as the church allows itself to be managed by the world's principles, she can expect to run into problems with God. *He* is running the church and He will have it run *His way*! [Leaders] must consider it of prime importance, therefore, not to allow the church to be run strictly according to business principles. Businessmen in the congregation may clamor for more efficiency . . . but they must not (as a result) be allowed to reshape the church by the principles of business and management. The church must be shaped by her sovereign Lord![12]

Excellent spiritual leaders give much attention to managing the church with a style that is radically different from worldly principles of management. For example, leaders do not set goals for the congregation; rather, they help the church to set its own goals so that the church will grow in the process, own its goals, see them as worthwhile, and be motivated to achieve them. Paul prayed that the church would be able to discern what is best for itself (Phil. 1:9). Good leaders imitate that attitude. They do not say, "I know what is best for you" (even though they may know what is best). Rather, they say, "I want you to be spiritually discerning

11. Myron Rush, *Management: A Biblical Approach* (Wheaton: Victor, 1983), 11.
12. Jay Adams, *Shepherding God's Flock* (Grand Rapids: Baker, 1980), 336.

enough to decide what is best for yourselves." Leaders work to achieve that maturity in the church. Christian management style is characterized by loving service, patient understanding, and gentle guidance, not by a "running-the-show" mentality frequently found in corporate executives.

This management function of leaders means also that leaders do what the church cannot do for itself. Obviously, the church cannot operate effectively or efficiently by attempting to be a committee of the whole on every matter, or a pure democracy. Especially as the church increases in size, it is necessary to allow leaders to assume increasing responsibility for many tasks, some of which are very important. To involve the entire church in every necessary task or decision is unreasonable, impractical, impossible, and wasteful of time and talent. The purpose of leadership is to assume responsibility, to some extent as representatives in Congress assume responsibility for the country.[13]

Wise and effective churches delegate many administrative duties to their leaders and allow them to function in these capacties. Some churches are paranoid about their leaders becoming too powerful. They cripple their leadership by withholding from them the authority they need to fulfill their responsibilities.

Administrative Responsibility

Administration involves a whole cluster of responsibilities: planning, organizing, staffing, delegating, recommending, coordinating, evaluating, keeping records, and budgeting, to name a few.[14] These things are often routine but necessary functions and cannot normally be done by large groups. They can be accomplished only by small groups of leaders, or by gifted individuals. Again, it is questionable how many of these things pastors ought to do, or how much time pastors should give to them. However, other leaders should give time to these crucial functions.

Great care needs to be exercised in carrying out these functions,

13. The analogy, however, is not wholly accurate and should not be pushed too far. Citizens have no control over Congress except the power to remove them at the next election (and the power of public opinion). Congress also enacts laws governing all citizens, and so forth.
14. Many current books on management treat these subjects in considerable detail.

or it will appear that the leaders are "running the church," which they are not authorized to do.

An example is necessary. One of the functions of leaders is to plan. How do leaders plan so that they do not function as autocrats who make plans for the church and then tell the congregation what it must do? Effective leaders do not make plans for the congregation, but in conjunction with the congregation and under divine guidance. This requires leaders to seek divine guidance through Scripture and prayer and to lead the church to do the same. It also means that leaders must have their fingers on the pulse of the congregation, sample opinions of congregation members, solicit suggestions and ideas from the congregation, seek conflicting opinions, challenge the congregation to faith in making plans, evaluate feedback from the congregation on proposed plans, and work in harmony with decisions of other leaders and the congregation itself. Obviously, the more important the plans being made, the more important are all of these things. Simple, routine, daily plans do not require such extensive involvement of the congregation. Good leaders always make members feel a part of the process, not incidental or dispensable to the process. Thomas Gordon strikes the right note: "Effective leaders must behave in such a way that they come to be perceived almost as another group member; at the same time they must help all group members feel as free as the leader to make contributions and perform needed functions in the group."[15] This kind of management takes an extreme sensitivity to the feelings of people and to the Holy Spirit.

Leaders must never lose sight of the fact that the church is God's church; he is to be in control, and all plans must be his plans, accomplished in his way. Planning does not mean that leaders are laying their plans on the congregation. When the plans are completed it must be said, "These are the plans of the church and the desire of God which we will carry out together by his grace and with his help," not, "These are the plans of the leaders and the church is to carry them out." When major decisions are made, leaders and followers must be able to say, "It seemed good to the Holy Spirit and to us" (Acts 15:28).

Leaders may later identify specific activities to be performed in the carrying out of the plans after they are approved, perhaps de-

15. Thomas Gordon, *Leader Effectiveness Training* (New York: Wyden, 1977), 36.

cide their sequence, assemble resources required to accomplish them, and implement them in the church. All of this, too, must be done not in the spirit of a controller over the church, but with the spirit of a servant within the church and under the authority of Christ.

Effective leaders perform these management functions in a way that promotes trust on the part of the congregation. Congregations should empower their leaders to carry out management responsibilities and then trust them to fulfill those responsibilities in a godly, gracious, and diligent way. If leaders prove themselves untrustworthy or abusive of their authority, they should be removed from their positions by the congregation.

Often leaders begin their work with enthusiasm and dedication, but quickly lose their taste for the job because they find they do nothing but attend meetings; their decisions are reversed by congregations without sufficient reason; their recommendations are dismissed with nonchalant disregard; and their time is wasted. The problem has often been that leaders were not trusted by the congregation, sometimes (but not always) because they behaved in such a way that they did not deserve to be trusted.

This does not mean that congregations must rubber-stamp every proposal of leaders, nor does it mean that leaders must be given unlimited power to control. Rather, congregations must make sober, intelligent decisions about what responsibilities should be delegated to their leaders, select those leaders carefully according to obvious gifts and scriptural qualifications, and trust them to do their jobs for the welfare of the body. The congregation must also remove leaders who abuse their privileges. Leaders, for their part, must prove themselves trustworthy by not abusing leadership prerogatives.

Summary

It is difficult, perhaps impossible, always to recognize what makes some leaders effective and others ineffective. The business and political worlds tend to judge effectiveness by materialistic standards, primarily physical growth, profit, and power. Spiritual effectiveness is evaluated according to entirely different criteria.

Church leaders excel when, through their inspirational influence, the church's philosophy of ministry becomes clearly understood and operational in the constituency. Effective, ministering churches have leaders who know where the church is going, who help the church get there, and who make the mission seem important, possible, and exciting to the congregation.

Effectiveness may be further gauged by the leaders' contagious spirit of outreach. Excellent leaders see themselves and the church as ambassadors for Christ. Growing churches have a passion for evangelism, and behind that passion are leaders whose contagious spirit of outreach has infected others.

Lastly, effective leaders produce a healthy church body. The members of the church are equipped and functional in the work of the ministry. This means that leaders take seriously their responsibility to equip the saints, and they are willing to eliminate or change programs that are merely traditional. Leaders often initiate new plans, so that what is done produces gifted, mature, and ministering people. Discipleship ministry and leadership training are integral to leadership effectiveness.

Effective leaders efficiently administer the daily affairs of the church, not with the world's philosophy of management, but with a style that is distinctly Christian and biblical. It is questionable, however, to what extent pastoral leaders should be involved in administrative tasks. Pastors must not neglect their primary roles. Yet, pastors must do some administrative work, and they must do it well so that they will have time for their primary tasks of prayer, preaching-teaching-discipling, and shepherding.

Good leaders must be extremely sensitive to the feelings of people and to the Holy Spirit so that their management style demonstrates loving service to the body.

PART 3

Leadership and Decision Making in the Church

9

Leadership in Decision Making
Philosophy

All spiritual leaders have a basic philosophy of decision making. Whether or not it is conscious and articulated, this philosophy influences or controls leaders' actions in church decision making. There is an enormous behavioral difference between leaders who believe that the church should make major decisions with its leaders' guidance and those who believe that leaders should make major decisions for the church.

At this point, our discussion is not about church routine, the daily decisions—ordering supplies, directing staff, selecting a Sunday school teacher—that are clearly delegated (or ought to be) to leaders. Leaders must make many of these ordinary decisions for the church, and churches should trust their leaders to do so wisely. In varying degrees, churches entrust decision making to their leaders. However, significant decisions affecting the whole body are a major concern which leaders are wise not to control. The church should participate in crucial decisions such as adopting major policies, articulating church goals, incurring significant debt, purchasing or selling church property, launching a building program, approving an annual budget, and calling professional staff.

This entire book has focused on spiritual leadership philosophy. Now, however, we will examine the basic commitments for servant-leaders in helping groups make decisions. Leaders should have a clear perception of how church decisions are made, how change comes about, and the specific function of leadership in guiding these decisions. Without such understandings, leaders are apt to muddle along with little direction for their own behavior and little direction for the church.

The general rubric under which specific principles are subsumed is that leaders are to assist and guide the church in the decision-making process, but leaders are not to become dictators (not even benevolent dictators) who legislate major decisions for the church. The following distinctive commitments build upon this foundation.

A Rigorous Commitment to Scripture and Church By-Laws

The objective documents that control the church are Scripture and its own constitution with articles of incorporation and by-laws. Some churches also have a policy manual. Any proposed decision or change should be submitted to the test of Scripture and the self-approved documents of the church. Leaders must be controlled by these restrictions upon their actions. If the direction or proposed action of the church contradicts Scripture or those guidelines previously adopted by the congregation, the decisions must be restructured and brought into conformity with church guidelines. Leaders and churches sometimes get into serious trouble because they ignore these limitations upon their actions.

Of course, by-laws and policy manuals can be amended, and it is advisable to periodically review them to make them more accurate and functionally efficient. However, for leaders and churches to disregard their own guidelines is to place both leaders and constituents in untenable positions. Discord and frustration with decision making are sure to result. Amending basic church documents during a time of crisis or when a crucial decision is pending seldom works.

A Commitment to Group Process

The responsibilities of spiritual leaders are to stimulate the church to identify its real needs, motivate the church to change so that its goals may be met, and guide the church in making decisions that are compatible with its approved guidelines, particularly scriptural guidelines. Leaders facilitate church decision making, but do not dictate decisions to the church. All of this involves group process, not unilateral action of leaders.

The function of church leaders is not to make decisions for the church, unless they are decisions properly delegated to them by the church. Leaders do not hand down major decisions for the body to carry out. Larry Richards and Clyde Hoeldtke may have overstated this principle to some degree, but essentially they are correct: "Elders are not to make decisions for others in the body: they are to affirm Christ as the head. What elders *can* do is give insight, suggestions, support, and sometimes advice to help the responsible parties make good decisions."[1]

Of course, some leaders and ecclesiastical traditions disagree with this stance. The foundational beliefs of such traditions suggest that the church is incapable of making good decisions for itself, that churches are inefficient in decision making, and that, therefore, leaders must make all decisions for the church.

A healthy leadership philosophy suggests that leadership domination of major church decisions usurps the headship of Christ, denigrates human dignity, and is incompatible with scriptural teaching. The same principle is valid for leaders operating with boards or committees. Excessive use of authority is prohibited. What is or is not excessive inevitably varies in the thinking and definitions of leaders, but leaders must be sensitive both to the teaching of Scripture and to the feelings and perceptions of their constituencies. Leaders seldom are effective or remain leaders for long if they are oblivious to the feelings of followers. Moreover, leadership control of church decisions is ineffective (though often efficient) because excessive use of authority creates hostility, servility, or both. Many leaders opt for short-term efficiency over long-term effectiveness, but often come to regret it.

Spiritual servant-leaders take responsibility to serve the church

1. Larry Richards and Clyde Hoeldtke, *A Theology of Church Leadership* (Grand Rapids: Zondervan, 1980), 309.

by helping it to set and achieve worthy goals, as Grace Elliott states clearly:

> The responsibility of the *designated leader* . . . is not primarily to provide directives but to maintain the evocative situation. Though he may be relatively conspicuous, he need not dominate. His role is crucial in keeping the goal in sight, creating a warm and permissive atmosphere for participation, recognizing consensus, helping persons find their parts in cooperative effort, keeping deliberations on the track toward decision.[2]

In carrying out these functions, leaders must refuse to usurp responsibilities that belong to Christ and to the church. Paul wrote to the church, "Find out what pleases the Lord" (Eph. 5:10); he did not say to the leaders, "Find out what is good for the congregation; tell them what to do; and see that they do it." The church has its own responsibility, and leaders must refuse to accept duties that belong to the church as a whole, even if the church desires them to take such responsibilities. To do so is to functionally cripple the church and make it unduly dependent.

In view of these comments, a statement by Ted Engstrom is disconcerting: "When a leader is sure of the will of God and the right course of action, he is able immediately to make a decision regardless of the circumstances."[3] There is no problem with this if the decision affects only the leader or has been delegated specifically to the leader, but in the context of church decisions it becomes the antithesis of team concept, collegiality in ministry, group responsibility, leadership training, and an appropriate leadership responsibility. A Christian leader is seldom, if ever, "sure of the will of God and the right course of action" for other people, unless that certainty is specifically revealed in Scripture. Further, such a position denies the freedom of the local church to be involved in making decisions under Christ that affect its own future. The words *regardless of the circumstances* in Engstrom's comment are particularly troubling.

In all significant changes in the church, leaders must work with

2. Grace Elliott, *How to Help Groups Make Decisions* (New York: Association, 1959), 42.

3. Ted Engstrom, *The Making of a Christian Leader* (Grand Rapids: Zondervan, 1976), 116.

followers toward shared goals. Leaders enlist members, elicit their contributions, inspire their performance, and resist usurping the authority of Christ or the authority of the church. All of this involves a commitment to group process.

A Commitment to Encourage Debate

Closely related to encouraging group process is the leader's commitment to solicit conflicting opinion. Effective servant-leaders do not discourage the free exchange of ideas; they encourage debate in the belief that better decisions are made by a group of people interacting than by individuals acting alone. Good leaders also are committed to the principle that groups function best and are more unified when each member feels the liberty to participate, debate, and exchange ideas without fear of ridicule or punishment. No one's opinions, ideas, suggestions, or constructive criticisms are thought worthless. Group thinking and group-established goals lie at the heart of group-centered leadership that is antidemagogic.

> Planned community change calls for effective leaders who are committed to the task and who give continuous guidance to the process. Leadership of the change process is essentially a matter of providing opportunities for *group* thinking, because most changes come about only if leaders are able to muster the support of community groups that have thought through what is involved.[4]

A worthy leadership philosophy never allows for slighting members, never discourages dissent, and never ridicules objectors. Healthy conflict is regarded as beneficial to the process. "Planned community change calls for the release and utilization of the contributions of *all* interested individuals and groups. Discussion, deliberation, and decision-making about important community changes must be open and forthright. The more people involved, the better the chance the change has of being legislated and accepted."[5] Poor church leaders try to squelch opposition, circumvent dissenters, and railroad legislation.

Of course, groups do not always make good decisions, just as

4. Harleigh Trecker and Audrey Trecker, *Working with Groups, Committees, and Communities* (Chicago: Follett, 1979), 205.
5. Ibid., 206.

leaders do not always make good decisions. Fallible people err as individuals and as groups. However, this does not invalidate the following sound principles:

1. Group members should participate in major decisions that affect themselves.
2. Groups are likely to make better decisions than individuals.
3. Healthy debate is a profitable endeavor and leads to better group decisions. Expressed difference of opinion is a positive influence in decision making.
4. Involved people do not feel disenfranchised; they are more committed to the decision after it is made when consensus is achieved.

For further treatment of this subject, leaders interested in group decision making should read Austin J. Freeley, *Argumentation and Debate* (Belmont, Calif.: Wadsworth, 1981) and Douglas Ehninger and Wayne Brockridge, *Decision by Debate* (New York: Dodd, Mead, 1963).

A Commitment to Consensus

Excellent leaders work patiently toward consensus, not majority vote, on major church decisions or important small-group decisions. There is often confusion about consensus. It is idealistic to think that absolute unanimity can always be achieved in a local church. Consensus has more to do with unity, accord, and harmony than it does the size of the vote. The significance of consensus lies in the degree of personal commitment that people feel toward a decision after it is reached.

Consensus means general agreement that a group's decision is the one that comes as close as possible to meeting the needs of everyone. Because there is such agreement, a truly sizable majority can support it with enthusiasm. In almost every consensus there will be people who would make a different decision if they had their preference. Nonetheless, most of those people feel that the compromise is satisfactory when it is worked out through a proper process of group participation. Often, people really do not insist on having their way, but they desperately want to be heard and resent being railroaded.

A mere vote does not always reveal whether consensus is achieved. There may be only a 60 percent vote for an issue, yet there may be considerable consensus if the 40 percent who vote against it are able to commit themselves to the decision because they recognize an appropriate compromise has been reached and everyone has had a genuine part in the decision. On the other hand, there may be a 90 percent vote for an issue with very little consensus, if many of the 90 percent vote as they do because they feel intimidated and if the 10 percent remain vigorously opposed to the decision. The size of a vote is not always a true indication of consensus or the lack of it. If the goodwill of a sizable proportion of the group is lost, consensus is lacking regardless of the vote. Leaders must be careful and sensitive about what interpretation they give to a congregational vote.

It is important that leaders recognize that the more important the decision and the more dramatic the proposed change, the more necessary consensus becomes. This is especially true for policy-making decisions that involve the values of the constituency. To fail to achieve consensus on important policy-making issues is to face an unacceptable risk of destroying unity, which frequently leads to the loss of members or a split in the church.

Poor leaders are too impatient, and perhaps too lazy, to work hard for consensus. Yet, consensus surely is what Scripture means by the words *one accord:*

> This is the heart of consensus. The team of responsible persons, honestly exploring a decision to be made, using all the capacities God has given them, and prayerfully seeking His will, *come to one accord.* When that accord has been achieved, when there is consensus, then the responsible group can move ahead with confidence that the direction in which they go does reflect the will of the Lord.[6]

Many churches suffer tragically because leaders are not willing to undertake the sometimes laborious, time-consuming task of achieving consensus. Others are determined to settle for nothing but their personal preference.

Good decisions on sensitive issues are not usually made; they evolve over time, through discussion and, often, through intense debate. The evolution of a good decision affecting many people

6. Richards and Hoeldtke, *A Theology of Church Leadership*, 307.

takes effort, much participation, and time; on major issues action without consensus is probably premature.

> In voluntary organizations . . . a simple majority is often not enough to make a decision that will be binding on all parties. . . . Any decision for a major change in a voluntary association normally requires the support of a consensus, not simply 50 percent plus one, if it is to be implemented effectively and without disruptive consequences. When this generalization is ignored the consequences may be both surprising and disruptive.[7]

There is always the possibility that consensus cannot be achieved regardless of the patience and diligent work of leaders. Usually this means that the status quo must be maintained, and leaders must wait patiently for changes in attitudes or circumstances. There are times when leaders must start over in the work of teaching, encouraging, and motivating before the church is adequately prepared to form a consensus on a major question.

Sometimes, however, to make no decision or merely to maintain the status quo is unacceptable to leaders; then leaders must decide whether it is worth the risk to resort to simple majority voting. Such moments are some of the most dangerous times in the life of the church, and extraordinary spiritual perceptivity is needed by those concerned for church welfare. Generally, a majority vote on a rather simple problem-solving issue is worth the risk of voting; issues in which people have strong emotional bias are not worth the risk, unless the matter is of compelling importance and there is a clear biblical mandate. The consequences of the lack of consensus for problem-solving tasks are generally not serious; the consequences of significant division about policy-making tasks are likely to be disastrous. We must recognize that even a church division is sometimes, though rarely, necessary. Certain doctrinal and moral principles cannot be compromised.

A Commitment to Discourage Voting

Good leaders recognize that voting rarely, if ever, contributes to consensus; it usually polarizes a group of people and is antithetical to group cohesiveness.

7. Lyle E. Schaller, *The Decision-Makers* (Nashville: Abingdon, 1974), 22.

A suggestion to discourage voting may seem surprising to many readers because *Robert's Rules of Order* has become nearly sacred in our democratic society. However, we must remember that such rules are not God's rules; they have been drafted by fallible people for the purpose of expediting business rather than achieving consensus.

Accepted parliamentary procedure has a place in the church because some procedural guidelines need to be followed, and the aforementioned guidelines are good as far as they go. If it is correctly and sensitively followed, parliamentary procedure gives an orderly opportunity for members to speak out, make motions, amend motions, and participate in decision making. However, formal parliamentary procedures may be suitable for routine, problem-solving types of issues, but inappropriate for other types of situations or questions that the church must resolve. Parliamentary procedure may serve to expedite business, but it can also be used to silence critics, squelch dissent, limit debate, and frustrate the process of achieving consensus.

Many organizations are not concerned about achieving consensus. For instance, the United States Congress is not normally interested in achieving consensus. Muscle, not consensus, rules supreme in Washington. If a sufficient number of votes can be mustered to pass a law or override a veto, seldom is anybody concerned about the feelings of the minority. Winners congratulate themselves, and losers lick their wounds and regroup to fight another day. It ought to be obvious that churches are wise to operate by a different set of principles.

Voting is a division of the house and, as such, it is the very thing the church does not want to do. Voting is a power play that allows the majority to inflict its will on the minority. That is a coarse but accurate assessment. Such polarization may seem necessary in certain situations, harmless, and even appropriate, but at other times it destroys the unity of the church and is counterproductive to healthy church goals.

Furthermore, the majority is not always right; the minority is often right (assuming there is a "right" on an issue, which is often debatable), and it becomes disruptive for the majority to suggest, as it frequently does, that God's will is reflected in the majority opinion. Some wise people have suggested that God's will is often revealed to a small minority who are out of step with the over-whelming majority.

All of this is not to say that parliamentary procedure should be thrown out entirely or that a vote should never be taken. Rather, great care should be exercised so that consensus is given time to develop through discussion, conflicting opinions, and debate, particularly on important and sensitive issues. No issue should be voted on prematurely, and some matters should not be voted on at all. Leaders should always remember that voting tends to harden opposing sides; voting seldom contributes to unity or consensus.

Of course, consensus is no guarantee of a good decision. Entire groups are wrong at times. God sometimes gives insight to one person or to a small group of members who stand opposed to the consensus of the body. All of this is true; it is also true that it is extremely difficult to implement important changes without broad support. There are never any guarantees of "rightness" in church decision making unless there is an unequivocal biblical mandate for the decision. Even those who form a sizable consensus must not be smugly satisfied that an issue has been rightly decided, especially when there are spiritually mature people who remain opposed.

Many leaders falsely believe that there are no alternatives to voting. Voting has become such an acceptable way of doing business that to oppose it sounds like heresy. Leaders should be challenged to explore other methods of decision making. Em Griffin's "Four Ways to Make Group Decisions" is a good place for leaders to begin a study of this important subject.[8]

A Commitment to Accept Compromise

Sometimes leaders are judged to be strong because they stand unequivocally for certain opinions, argue passionately for them, and never abandon them. Firm convictions on major doctrinal or moral issues may be praiseworthy, especially when leaders have clear scriptural teaching upon which to base their position. However, for most matters before the church, such inflexibility is a serious, often fatal, mistake.

Strong leaders are able and willing to compromise, admit error,

8. Em Griffin, "Four Ways to Make Group Decisions," *Leadership* (Spring 1982): 75.

change their opinions because of new data or argument, and achieve an acceptable consensus on sensitive issues.

> Solving problems and reaching decisions demand a kind of give-and-take where positions are at stake and where it is impossible for everyone concerned to be equally right all the time. But having to give way or to alter a position in the face of compelling argument is no loss. The executive who can develop a position, believe in it, support it to its fullest, and then back down is a strong person.[9]

Often we are conditioned to think that compromise is a dirty word. In reality, compromise is often a necessity in church decision making. Most decisions made by the church are not right or wrong decisions, but merely better or worse alternatives, or choices between two sets of problems. Leaders who are so stubborn that they are unwilling to accept and negotiate compromise cannot excel in Christian leadership. Ted W. Engstrom wisely observes:

> When we are young, we *refuse* to compromise. As we grow older, we realize we *have* to compromise. Perhaps in our thirties, we *learn* to compromise. By forty, we are *willing* to compromise. Sometime in life we (it is to be hoped) learn that often our "ideals" were less than ideal when placed alongside those of others. "*Our* goals" turn out to be more desirable than "*my* goals."[10]

The best decision on a policy-making issue is almost always a compromise between the extreme positions of opposing sides, one that necessitates that everyone yield some ground. The alternative to compromise is for one group to win and the other to lose. Winners typically feel smugly satisfied that they have prevailed, that they have defeated the opposition, and that they are right because they have won. Losers often feel defeated and in the wrong—failures at determining God's will. Good leaders recognize the value of negotiation, of reaching a decision where people do not feel that they have won or lost. In a compromise few people get exactly what they want, but there is general recognition that the best decision possible has been reached. Churchmanship is not a com-

9. Abraham Zaleznik, *Human Dilemmas of Leadership* (New York: Harper and Row, 1966), 36.

10. Ted W. Engstrom and Edward Dayton, *The Christian Executive* (Waco: Word, 1979), 59.

petitive sport. If some win and others lose, the body loses. Cooperation, unity, and a good decision necessitate compromise, particularly on sensitive issues.

Obviously, this discussion is not about compromising essential scriptural truth or clear moral standards. It is self-evident that these are not to be compromised. Rather, compromise in this context refers to decision making on difficult issues for which there are no clear biblical guidelines.

A Commitment to Both Facts and Feelings

Good, spiritual church leaders take into account both facts and feelings in the decision-making process. Poor leaders base decisions merely on facts or on feelings. Leaders who are the executive type tend to pride themselves on their objectivity, their ability to be cool, rational, and impartial in their analysis of facts. However, such a tendency may cause church leaders to ignore or overlook what are sometimes the most important facts of all: people's feelings, emotions, prejudices, and value systems.

Many decisions look theoretically right to leaders, but they are offensive to many people in the congregation. Such decisions may win a simple majority vote, but not the support of those who must implement them. Good leaders are not merely concerned with getting a decision, but with the practical implementation of the decision after it is made. Many leaders have congratulated themselves upon leading the church to make a certain decision, usually by majority vote, but then found that the decision could not be implemented because of the disunity that remained in the congregation. Perhaps such leaders fail to respect the feelings of the people. Leaders who scorn public opinion often wake to reality too late to salvage their leadership role. John W. Gardner observed that President Nixon, during the Vietnam war, was quite cognizant and realistic about the objective facts of troop strength, weapons, and the logistics of fighting, but unreceptive to the more subjective facts involving public rejection of the war.[11] Such insensitivity is often fatal to leadership.

On the other hand, to ignore objective facts in favor of merely

11. John W. Gardner, *Leadership and Power* (Washington, D.C.: Independent Sector, 1986), 11.

sampling public sentiment will also lead to poor decisions. Good leaders do not ride the wind of public opinion, but they are aware and respectful of it. Leadership is not simply jumping on the bandwagon of the majority. Some leaders are so fearful of offending someone that they are paralyzed into inaction.

Decision making in the church must not be forced to an either-or choice between people's value systems and more objective criteria for decision making. Rather, some important facts to consider, among other things, are individual and group feelings and value systems. The logic of the head and the logic of the heart are equally essential for spiritual leadership. The logic of the heart may seem irrational at times, but it is real and it is a potent force in the church. It can be ignored only at great peril.

High-powered executive types often have little patience with value systems, ingrained prejudices, or emotional bias. That's one reason why successful businessmen do not always make the best church leaders. Hard heads and soft hearts are not always found in the same person, but good church leadership demands both. Hard heads may evaluate objective facts with expertise, but it takes soft hearts to be sensitive to people's feelings.

For example, leaders sometimes want to tear down or sell an antiquated building for many good, objective reasons that are clear and irrefutable to them, but they fail to grasp the emotional attachment of the people to the building that was built by their parents and where they were baptized and married. Ignoring people's deeply ingrained sentiments can destroy church unity. This doesn't mean that the old church cannot be torn down or sold if necessary, but it does mean that leaders must be patient and respectful of feelings, must allow time for consensus to form, must make some compromises, and must be sensitive in guiding the church toward such a difficult decision.

Summary

Difficult decisions that affect the whole church require sensitive and earnest leaders. Good servant-leaders have a distinct philosophy of leadership behavior in church decision making and a number of basic commitments that serve them in their guidance of the church. The following commitments are suggested:

1. Leaders are committed to the Scripture and the documents adopted by the congregation.
2. Leaders are committed to assist the church or group in decision making; they are enablers, not commanders. They do not usurp the responsibilities of the church or group in making major decisions that affect the entire body. Leaders work with and for the group in decision making; the group does not work for the leaders.
3. Leaders are committed to group process, to the encouragement of debate, and to the involvement of members as much as possible and as is feasible in decision making.
4. Leaders are committed to achieving consensus, not mere majority vote. Consensus is revealed in the degree of commitment to the decision after it has evolved through discussion and compromise.
5. Leaders are committed to discouraging premature voting, and they understand that some matters should never be voted upon by the church. Voting is a division of the body and often destroys group cohesiveness.
6. Leaders are committed to negotiate and accept compromise on sensitive issues for which there is no clear biblical mandate.
7. Leaders are committed to a careful evaluation of both objective facts and subjective feelings. Poor church leaders are unbalanced in favor of objectivity or subjectivity, facts or feelings.

10

Leadership in Decision Making
Errors

One of the most difficult responsibilities of church leaders is to help their churches make important decisions that inevitably involve change. Spiritual leaders need extraordinary wisdom and spiritual perceptivity to lead the body effectively in decision making.

Every organization tends to maintain the status quo, or worse, to stagnate and deteriorate. The church resists change not only in its forms, structure, and government, but also in its methodology and especially in its traditions. "But we've always done it this way" are the words that characterize the typical church member.

Spiritual leaders who are eager for change in the church frequently meet with fierce resistance. Many pastors can remember the painful experience of trying to get even seemingly simple decisions enacted (e.g., changing the time of the Sunday morning worship service by fifteen minutes). Leaders who begin their ministries with a "take charge" attitude rapidly become disillusioned with what they perceive as obstinacy in their congregations. They generally underestimate how much people dislike change and resent the use of leadership authority, particularly by young, inexperienced leaders who have not earned congregational trust and goodwill. Seminary graduates who go out to serve their first churches are often shocked and frustrated when they encounter resistance to ideas that involve change.

When leaders press for decisions that involve change, people may become vocal and antipathic dissenters. Some passively resist, and others withdraw quietly (or not so quietly) from the church. It is not uncommon for people to leave a church because a relatively minor decision displeased them. Others express their resistance to change by withholding their tithes or gifts. Change that is unilaterally instituted by leaders is often resented even more, especially in churches that tenaciously hold to forms of government stressing congregational authority.

Another problem with church decision making is that leaders who have sufficient authority to effect change by their own action may find that the members become too dependent upon them, expecting the leaders to resolve every problem. Deference to leaders can become extreme and destructive. Sometimes leaders run the church as managers run a business. This may be flattering to the leaders, who appear extraordinarily efficient, but eventually it is damaging to the church. Some churches have forceful, dynamic people in office, but the leaders have erred in creating a church that merely acquiesces to pressure tactics or to the unilateral action of its leaders. Such churches may be numerically strong, but functionally weak.

Authoritarian leaders have often produced feeble followers. A church filled with submissive people is not a worthy goal. To make matters worse, sometimes leaders mistake compliance for unity, acquiescence for cohesiveness. Good leaders produce strong, contributing people, not weak, compliant people. The converse is also true. Able, participating constituents generally make for good leaders. Sometimes there are qualities in followers which invite the abuse of authority by leaders. Bertrand de Jouvenel said, "A society of sheep must in time beget a government of wolves." Obviously, the word *sheep* in this context is neither flattering nor biblical.

In spite of the difficulties and dangers associated with decision making, decisions to change both structures and methodologies must be made as needed to produce and maintain spiritual vitality. The only decisions some churches make are decisions to preserve the status quo. Such decisions really are decisions guaranteeing stagnation and deterioration.

The failure of leaders to lead the church to decisions and to stimulate change inevitably results in weak, ineffective, crippled church congregations. Conversely, a stunted, stagnant church is usually the result of poor leadership. Decay generally begins with the failure of leadership, not with the failure of constituency.

Leaders who have sufficient authority and control can make decisions unilaterally; they can simply direct changes to be made and enforce their decisions. For example, the owner and manager of a business usually can make changes without consulting or gaining the consent of his employees, unless a union has sufficient power to control certain changes. The president of a corporation is empowered to hand down directives which he expects to be carried out by his subordinates. Those who do not conform to the new orders may be demoted or terminated. No one in the church has or ought to have that kind of authority; such authority rests with Christ, and leaders must not usurp his place. Consequently, decision making and effecting change in a volunteer organization such as the church can be a frustrating, time-consuming, laborious, and dangerous process, particularly for leaders who by nature are aggressive people who get impatient with slow progress. Many church officers become totally frustrated with the whole business, give up the hope of change, and settle down to a dull maintenance ministry.

Many church leaders make serious, often fatal (in terms of continuing ministry), errors in their attempts to bring about decisions that will effect change. Numerous churches have divided in controversy over the wrenching experience of decision making or over leaders who are perceived to have behaved inappropriately in the process of getting decisions.

Often leaders themselves do not understand why they have failed, wondering, "Why didn't the church do what I suggested? I had great plans and expectations, but nobody paid attention." Leaders excuse their own failures, suggesting that the stubbornness and obstinacy of the constituency is the real problem. There are leaders who never entertain the thought that they could be the obstacle to effective church decisions.

Fundamental Orientation of Leadership

One of two fundamental attitudes is usually behind all that leaders do. First, there is the orientation that characterizes leaders who truly believe they know what the church should do. The more convinced these leaders are that they know and are right, the more they tend to exert pressure upon others to conform to their goals, yield to their opinions, and act according to their directives.

Few things are more dangerous in the church than leaders who are convinced that they alone know the right thing for other people to do. Such people almost always attempt a style of leadership (though they usually deny it) that pressures people to yield to their convictions. If their efforts meet with resistance, greater pressure is used. More quickly than they realize, they are perceived to be authoritarian, unethical, and manipulative. Resentment tends to build quickly in this situation.

One of the numerous problems with this whole orientation is that pressure tactics which may be effective in accomplishing the leader's objectives are incompatible with what the leader must achieve in interpersonal relationships.

There is a well-established maxim in the study of human behavior that describes this situation tersely and even poetically: "Love flees authority." Where one individual has the capacity to control and affect the actions of another, either by virtue of differences in their positions, knowledge, or experience, then the feeling governing the relationship tends to be one of distance, and perhaps respect, but not one ultimately of warmth and friendliness.[1]

Spiritual leaders must be perceived as trustworthy, warm, friendly, and loving, not merely as skilled, knowledgeable, or competent. Church leaders are not building a corporate enterprise; they are building a loving fellowship of believers. The creation of distance between leaders and followers defeats the purposes that characterize spiritual leadership. Unless there is warmth in spiri-

1. Abraham Zaleznik, *Human Dilemmas of Leadership* (New York: Harper and Row, 1966), 34.

tual leadership, leaders will easily be perceived as manipulative or high-handed, or they may gain mere subservience from their followers. It is difficult to be seen as both an authority figure and a spiritual shepherd. Those who insist on being an authority figure, with the dominance and control that such an image conveys, generally sacrifice a warm and loving relationship. As the maxim indicates, "Love flees authority."[2]

Second, there is the orientation of leaders who really believe and say, "I do not have all the answers, but I am committed to helping this body of believers to decide what we should do together in fulfilling the will of God in this community." Such leaders are not as likely to use methodologies that are perceived as unethical or manipulative. They also lay a foundation for spiritual shepherding, trusting relationships, and group cohesiveness.

This latter orientation characterizes leaders who are servant-leaders. Their leadership style, unlike that of autocrats, may be somewhat less efficient and more time-consuming, but it is more certain and effective because of the cohesiveness and consensus achieved in the church. This type of leader builds the trust in interpersonal relationships that is fundamental to healthy church fellowship. Again, John W. Gardner is absolutely correct: "Leaders must not only forge bonds of trust between themselves and their constituents, they must create a climate of trust throughout the system over which they preside. Trust is not the only glue that holds a human group together, but when it dissolves, the capacity of the group to function effectively is seriously impaired."[3]

Of course, some domineering and benevolent autocratic leaders gain the blind trust, and even the adoration, of their followers, despite their style. They seem to defy the rule about love fleeing authority. Again, however, it must be observed that such autocrats are exceptions, not the rule. In addition, their followers are in danger of becoming servile, not capable, church members.

Spiritual leaders must constantly be reminded that to fail in relationships and to alienate people is to fail in that which is vital

2. Again, this is not to say that spiritual leaders have no authority. There is great authority in the presentation of God's Word, as in the apostle Paul's ministry. Such authoritative ministry, however, is quite a different context than that discussed in this chapter.

3. John W. Gardner, *The Heart of the Matter: Leader-Constituent Interaction* (Washington, D.C.: Independent Sector, 1986), 18.

to continuing ministry with those people. To fail in relationships negates even the most spectacular of gifts and abilities. Relationships precede ministry; ministry necessitates relationships; and failed relationships preclude effective ministry. The warm, loving relationship between spiritual leaders and their followers is essential, not optional. Surely Paul had this in mind when he wrote:

> If I speak in the tongues of men and of angels, but have not love, I am only a resounding gong or a clanging cymbal. If I have the gift of prophecy and can fathom all mysteries and all knowledge, and if I have a faith that can move mountains, but have not love, I am nothing. If I give all I possess to the poor and surrender my body to the flames, but have not love, I gain nothing. . . . [1 Cor. 13:1–3]

A lay elder in a large metropolitan church spoke of the qualities of his pastor. A number of complimentary things were said, and then the elder added, "but, [long pause] he's not a loving man." The lay leader did not realize the implication of what he said. Such an indictment neutralized all of the positive things expressed. Spiritual leaders must be loving and caring people or whatever they do is likely to be perceived as the manipulative, shrewd maneuvering of an ambitious leader.

Sometimes the assertion is made that occasionally it is necessary for leaders to alienate people and that even Paul (and many Old Testament prophets) made enemies. Of course, this is true, but we must remember that not even Paul could continue ministry with those he alienated. Further, abrasiveness did not characterize Paul's relationship with his churches. The alienation of unbelievers is often unavoidable, but spiritual shepherds must do everything possible to avoid ruptures within their own church body.

There are those times when the leader must take unpopular positions for the sake of conscience or principles that cannot be compromised. John Adams is reported to have said to Congress on one occasion: "Let us not be palsied by the will of our constituents." Such leaders must be prepared for martyrdom or, at least, the termination of ministry in that place.

Creating distance in interpersonal relationships is the antithesis of the biblical pattern for service to the church. Like it or not, the effectiveness of leaders depends largely upon the degree to which they are accepted, respected, trusted, and loved by the people.

This is why a primary responsibility, perhaps the first responsibility, of a Christian leader is to earn the love and respect of the congregation, the right to be heard and the right to lead.

Errors of Leadership in Effecting Change

It is crucial that leaders understand the dynamics of their own behavior in the decision-making process. When leaders resign in frustration or under pressure, and when churches splinter with bitter recriminations against their leaders, leaders generally have failed to behave appropriately in bringing about decisions. Most likely leaders have committed one or more of the following errors.

Leaders Press for Goals Not Owned by Members

Ownership of goals is crucial to their achievement and vital to the cohesiveness of the group. Churches are unlikely to develop or maintain unity if they are pushed to achieve goals which may be the leaders' goals, but which are not developed and shared by rank-and-file members.

One of the easiest things for leaders to do is to impose their own objectives (what seems right and good to them) on the church. Frequently, a sense of superiority causes leaders to feel that they alone have a direct pipeline to God and that God has revealed to them his will for the church. When this happens the leaders constantly find themselves trying to push, pull, drive, cajole, or maneuver the church into doing what they think ought to be done. People who are pushed to achieve what they have no desire to achieve usually develop antagonistic attitudes toward the leaders, which result in resistance or withdrawal.

Of course, the church may not have any goals of its own. Few churches do, as a matter of fact, unless they have been blessed with excellent leaders. If the church is without carefully worked out goals, it becomes easy for leaders (or any strong personality) merely to interject their own preference instead of going through the painstaking process of helping the church to identify its goals. When the process is short-circuited in this way, interpersonal tension is likely to become destructive. Further, if leaders succeed in getting their goals formally adopted, they may have brought about only acquiescence, not enthusiastic support.

Leaders Use Manipulative Methologies

Leaders, by their very nature, precede followers in seeing the need for change. Leaders are the first to recognize that a decision must be made to provide additional space, change unworkable policies, purchase different educational curricula, integrate minority groups, restate a doctrinal position, call additional staff, acquire overhead projectors, or relocate the church.

Leaders who desire that the church make decisions for change are always in danger of using methodologies that may or may not be effective in accomplishing their desires, but are counterproductive in terms of relationships. The greater the desire for change, the greater is the likelihood that leaders will use alienating methods to achieve the change. Increased temptation to use a manipulative or excessively aggressive methodology is in direct proportion to the increased desire for change on the part of leaders. A leader who passionately wants and believes in a certain change faces risk. Followers will resist manipulation with great zest and intensity.

Leaders Fail to Motivate People

One of the functions of leaders is to identify problems or needs and motivate people to recognize and resolve those problems and meet those needs. Leaders who attempt to prompt change before the congregation has sufficient motivation to change will inevitably meet resistance and, most likely, failure. People are not like cattle; they cannot be herded or driven to decisions, especially in volunteer organizations. They must be shepherded and led gently. They must be respected as individuals who are thinking, feeling human beings. In leading, as opposed to pushing, motivation is vital.

As previously noted, good leaders almost always see the need for change before followers do. This is an essential part of leadership and vision. Without the recognition of needs, no one can lead. However, leaders with great vision tend to be impatient. They want to see something done now, not a month or a year from now. Consequently, leaders often by-pass the sometimes agonizing, time-consuming process of teaching, encouraging, and motivating their constituency. They fail to understand that only when the church has grasped the concept that changes are necessary, possible, and desirable, and when the people themselves are excited and motivated to work and give, can the right decisions be made safely and effectively. "Perhaps the most promising trend in our thinking about leadership is the growing conviction that the purposes of the group are best served when the leader helps followers to develop their own initiative, strengthens them in the use of their own judgment, enables them to grow and to become better contributors."[4]

When good leaders have accomplished their motivational responsibilities and have stimulated people to recognize need and to desire change, the leaders are in position to help the church discover what specific changes need to be made, what the church goals should be, and what decisions will lead to the accomplishment of those goals. This kind of leadership is difficult, demanding, and often time-consuming. It calls for delicacy, wisdom, patience, and spiritual discernment. It is no job for the novice. Leaders who short-circuit the process by pushing prematurely for important decisions often find themselves shoved to the sidelines by people who will not be shoved.

Leaders Fail to Assess Group Capacities

Good spiritual leaders must have the wisdom to understand the capacities for achievement by the church. When leaders encourage, push, or otherwise help the church to adopt goals which are not within their capabilities to achieve, even with hard work and faith, the congregation eventually becomes frustrated and, possibly, embittered.

Sometimes, in their zeal to accomplish great plans, leaders fail to grasp reality. Good goals must be both specific and attainable. Poor leaders lead people to develop plans which, in spite of great faith and sacrifice, the church is not able to realize. When this happens, congregations get disillusioned with their leaders and think, "Who got us into this mess?" The words of Jesus are a potent reminder: "Suppose one of you wants to build a tower. Will he not first sit down and estimate the cost to see if he has enough money to complete it? For if he lays the foundation and is not able to finish it, everyone who sees it will ridicule him, saying, 'This fellow began to build and was not able to finish' " (Luke 14:28–30).

Good spiritual leaders estimate the cost (not merely the financial cost) of all proposed plans and determine accurately whether the

4. Ibid., 23.

congregation has the spiritual, financial, and physical capacities to achieve what is being projected. They help churches adopt goals and plans that are possible to attain with faith, sacrifice, and hard work. Leaders who are so idealistic or visionary that they are determined to lead the church down impossible roads are likely to find themselves without a following.

Leaders Fail to Enlist Essential People

Good leaders know that in any volunteer body such as the church there are comparatively few people whose encouragement, support, and finances are crucial to the process of decision making and action. These people are estimated to be between 12 and 17 percent of the total congregation. They typically are respected individuals who frequently hold offices, teach classes, and speak out in church business meetings. Church leaders must know who they are and how influential they are. Other people will usually follow along if they know that this nucleus supports a proposed action.

It is usual for very few people to have enormous influence in the church. They may not be officers of the church or in any position of formal leadership, but they are powerful people nevertheless. If leaders make the mistake of attempting to lead the church to major decisions involving significant change while circumventing these influential people, they are likely to fail. Good leaders are realistic about the dynamics of people power within the organization. Ignorance or indifference to the power structures of the church ensures failure.

If decisions are made unilaterally by leaders or by a small, select group of officers, and then influential people are solicited to go along with the decisions, a serious question of propriety arises. Leaders must then resort to playing politics to secure people's support for what already has been decided. It is not unusual for such tactics to backfire.

Rather than involving highly respected people after the fact (that is, after the decision), these people whose support is so crucial must be involved in the whole process of goal setting, decision making, and change. It is advantageous to encourage people to participate in all the various phases and to solicit their wisdom, expertise, and counsel. Then, when decisions evolve and recommendations and consensus form in boards or committees, the leaders need not be concerned that these people have been overlooked.

When the congregation meets to review decisions or adopt recommendations, the leaders are not apt to be surprised by influential people who are hostile, possibly because they were ignored.

Leaders Fail to Grasp Group Dynamics

Most church leaders would profit greatly from a good university course in group dynamics and group process. Group dynamics has to do with the rise and fall, ebb and flow, of interpersonal relationships within the group. Group process is concerned with the procedure used to accomplish an agenda. Leaders must understand both process and dynamics, yet few leaders have had formal training in these subjects. Failure to understand group dynamics and process almost inevitably ensures leadership failure. When leaders fail to understand what is going on within the group, they often miss signs of group alienation, withdrawal, hostility to leadership, or group polarization. Poor leaders do not detect the body language, the tone of the voice, the faraway stare, the acid comment, or other clues that may indicate that a good decision is becoming increasingly unlikely because of the attitudes of the group. Poor leaders do not know when to slow down, retrace steps, elicit new opinions, stimulate presentation of different ideas, give a word of encouragement, suggest a compromise, postpone action, or reach out to nonparticipants. Hence, there is a lot of fumbling, wasted time, and general confusion. The result is fragmentation, a poor decision, or no decision at all.

Many times leaders do not know how good decisions evolve in groups, which decisions need consensus, and why some procedures are suitable for certain kinds of decisions but are unsuitable for others. Leaders who muddle along year after year with little to show for their efforts probably do not understand how change happens, how to lead groups to make decisions, or how group decisions are enacted or enforced. They do not understand what groups need from their leaders.

The effective leader is able to work with groups of people so as to help the various individuals in the group fulfill their own separate responsibilities needed for group achievement. Guidance, stimulation, interpretation, analysis, planning, and focusing seem to loom large in the leadership process. This does not mean that your role as a leader is any less dynamic. It means that you direct attention toward the group process and group product rather than toward your own achievements. The notion of helping or enabling as being central to the leadership process has another implication. The basic satisfactions accruing to the one who leads the group must be secured in new and different ways. "We did it" must have greater value than "I did it." The rewards for successful group leadership must be shared with the members.[5]

It is not the purpose of this book to provide a detailed explication of group dynamics or group process. Some of these topics will be discussed in the following chapters, but the serious student of group decision making should carefully read *Small Group Decision Making* for an excellent discussion of both prescriptive and descriptive models of decision making and for an examination of the process of decision emergence.[6]

Good church leaders encourage group members to express themselves and to participate with others in the process. They do not reject or minimize the contributions of church members. Leaders ask questions to elicit the opinions of others. They define and sometimes redefine problems or questions to help people to know precisely where the group is headed. They help the group move on to a new stage of thinking when it becomes bogged down. Leaders provide the group with direction without domineering. They inspire members to believe that they can and will perform capably and make good decisions. They make sure that the group devotes time to systematically evaluating itself. They see to it that the meeting is drawn to a close with a good summary of what has been done and what lies ahead in the decision-making process.

All of these things are essential ingredients of good leadership in church decision making. Leaders who do not understand these elements of group dynamics and process are likely to fail.

Summary

One of the most difficult responsibilities of church leaders is to help their churches make decisions to change. Organizations tend

5. Harleigh Trecker and Audrey Trecker, *Working with Groups, Committees, and Communities* (Chicago: Follett, 1979), 69.

6. B. Aubrey Fisher, *Small Group Decision Making: Communication and Group Process* (New York: McGraw-Hill, 1974). Also helpful are Dennis S. Gouran, *Discussion: The Process of Group Decision Making* (New York: Harper and Row, 1974); John Hasling, *Group Discussion and Decision Making* (New York: Thomas Y. Crowell, 1975); and Trecker and Trecker, *Working with Groups, Committees, and Communities*.

to stagnate and deteriorate, and churches, in particular, have been historically resistant to change. Decision making in the typical church with congregational polity is a difficult process. Unless leaders use great care and wisdom, they risk alienating members or creating little more than docile acquiescence in the church.

Leaders tend either to believe that they alone know what the church should do, or to be committed to helping the church decide what should be done to fulfill the will of God. The first orientation often leads to manipulative tactics. The second orientation is more compatible with the concept of servant-leadership.

Leaders who fail to help churches make major decisions involving change usually make one of the following errors:

1. Leaders attempt to move the church toward a goal that the members do not own. Ownership of goals is vital to the achievement of those goals.
2. Leaders use methodologies that are perceived as unprincipled or manipulative. People naturally resent being treated with disrespect or herded like cattle.
3. Leaders fail to motivate the church to change. Leaders are frequently impatient with the slowness of church decision making and tend to act prematurely.
4. Leaders fail to assess accurately the capacity of the church to change. Goals must be attainable by faith and hard work. Unattainable goals reflect poorly upon leaders.
5. Leaders fail to enlist individuals whose support is necessary. Comparatively few people have major influence, and unless these people are involved in the process and supportive of decisions it is unlikely that good decisions can be made and implemented.
6. Leaders fail to understand the dynamics of groups and the process of group decision making. Poor leaders do not detect the signals of group fragmentation, do not understand how decisions are made, and fail to assess accurately the need for encouragement, solicitation of fresh ideas, postponement of action, or implementation of a different procedure.

Spiritual leaders must avoid these errors if they are to effectively and efficiently lead churches to make necessary decisions involving significant change.

11

Leadership in Decision Making
Motivation

Leadership effectiveness depends upon the ability of leaders to stimulate others to make decisions involving change. As was noted in the previous chapter, attempts to motivate can easily become unethical, manipulative, or exploitative, and spiritual leaders need to be particularly aware of the morality of their motivational efforts. However, no one really is a leader who fails to inspire followers to make decisions and take action. Leadership is judged not by official position, but by progress made in the lives of followers.

Motivation is anything which determines volition or prompts a person or group to act in a certain way. Motivation is incentive, stimulus, that which moves people to do something. Of course, many things move people to take action, including the inner drives of the people themselves and the pressures of external circumstances. However, our concern is with the action of spiritual leaders that inspires the church to make corporate decisions to change.

Christian leaders must carefully guard against pragmatism in motivational technique. There is a temptation to think that a worthy end justifies any means of achieving it. An action is not justifiable just because it results in something desirable. Pragmatists believe that whatever produces a good result must be right, and whatever produces a bad result must be wrong. Such thinking raises serious questions about ethics.

Pragmatic techniques may win the battle (achieve a temporary objective), but eventually something far more valuable will be lost, namely, the credibility of the leaders themselves. For example, many pastors have used questionable, pressure-filled strategies to get churches to erect expensive buildings, but when the buildings were completed the pastors found it necessary to find ministries elsewhere. When people become alienated and the pastors lose credibility, dissension or hostility makes continued ministry impossible.

We observed in the previous chapter that the keener the desire on the part of leaders for decision and change, the greater is the temptation to utilize methodologies that may be questionable or unethical. One of the great challenges facing leaders is the need for scrutiny of their own motivations before they attempt to motivate others. If leaders are self-serving, they are likely to behave in a way that will cost them their integrity and esteem in the eyes of followers. When this happens in the church, leaders soon discover that they have no followers and wonder how it happened.

One theory of leadership suggests that people need pressure and coercion in order to be productive:

> The essence of the manager's task is to organize the human and non-human resources available to the organization that employs him so as to improve its position in the marketplace. His role is to persuade, inspire, manipulate, cajole, and intimidate those he manages so that his organization measures up to criteria of effectiveness shaped ultimately by the market but specifically by the expectations of those in control of his organization—finally, its owners.[1]

It ought to be self-evident that such a description of role and task does not fit a spiritual leader in Christian ministry.

The general framework under which spiritual leaders must work

---

1. Robert N. Bellah et al., *Habits of the Heart: Individualism and Commitment in American Life* (New York: Harper and Row, 1985), 45.

assumes that people want something better than they have yet achieved, they want their basic needs met, and they want leaders who will inspire them to become all that God intends them to be. These wants may be nonverbalized and perhaps unconscious, but they exist nevertheless. However, people do not want to be managed or manipulated; they want to be treated with respect—inspired but not coerced, motivated but not intimidated.

Many people, in spite of their resistance to change in the church, are tired of mediocrity. They long to be moved, not by pressure tactics, but by inspiring example, patient instruction, and loving care. People want and need spiritual shepherds who will lead them through the wilderness and to green pastures. They want the church to become a vital force, a spiritually robust, convincing reality within its community. They don't really want their church to be stagnant and spiritually dead. Not only do many people hunger for those things for their church, but also they want them for themselves, although many have probably given up hope of ever achieving them. Defeat has become a way of life for many professing Christians.

In all that leaders do, motivation is central. How do spiritual leaders stimulate people to action? What are the basic motivational methods that can either inspire or demoralize congregations?

Unworthy Motivational Tactics

Individual sensitivity to motivational techniques will inevitably differ. Some things that may be regarded as ethically proper by some leaders will be rejected by others, and vice versa. Some tactics are unacceptable for spiritual leaders. It will be up to the individual leader to agree or disagree with suggestions and to formulate a biblical, workable code of motivational ethics.

As a general rule, any motivational tactic that involves coercion is inappropriate for spiritual leaders. John Harris describes such tactics:

> This is the [leader's] assertion of power *over* others. It is unilateral influence by which the [leader] tries to reshape the basic consensus within the congregation. He decides what is to be done and how. He consciously works to give the appearance of not manipulating, yet at the same time carefully manages the strings of power. . . .

Proactive influence also may be less subtle, employing open coercion or heavy persuasion in a process of direct domination. In effect, the message picked up by the laity [followers] is: "You must do what I want because I have the power and knowledge to decide what's best for you." . . .It is hard to distinguish courageous forms of proactive influence from forms in which the [leader] is simply autocratic or pathologically willful.[2]

Those leaders who adopt such a managerial strategy make church decisions a win-lose game in which leaders are determined to win by exerting sufficient power to control process, church decisions, and people. The power may be that of superior knowledge or expertise, or it may be the power of personal charisma (a guru, of sorts), or it may be the accrued power of long tenure and respect. The bottom line of such strategy, however, is the use of power to coercively, though not always overtly, force action. This we hold to be contrary to Scripture, morally unacceptable, and beneath the dignity of spiritual leaders.

Some may immediately object and cite Jesus, who acted coercively in cleansing the temple, or Paul, who clearly pressured the Corinthian church by demanding the excommunication of a moral offender. We need to remember that Jesus was God and therefore possessed an authority that has no parallel with the spiritual authority of church leaders. For Jesus to act as he did was perfectly right and acceptable; for church leaders to behave as though they are God is inappropriate and offensive. Paul was an apostle, and as such, possessed an authority that not many of us can claim. If, however, this argument is rejected, we still must remind ourselves that Paul was absolutely confident of the will of God and declared to the Corinthian church the authoritative Word of God, not his personal, private opinion about church decisions. When spiritual leaders proclaim God's revealed Word, they must proclaim it with authority. That, however, is different from coercively pressuring the church to adopt the leaders' proposals, which certainly are not the authoritative Word of God.

What are the special motivational techniques that are subsumed under the banner of unacceptable, coercive methodology? We will disregard obvious unethical methods (lying, bribery, and threat,

2. John Harris, *Stress, Power, and Ministry* (Washington, D.C.: Alban Institute, 1979), 102–3.

for example) and note the following unscrupulous and unworthy tactics.

Appeal to Direct Revelation

The appeal to direct revelation is a popular motivational strategy used by some church leaders. These leaders tend to coerce people to conform to their will by suggesting (not always with subtlety) that God is on their side, that God has spoken to them directly, perhaps even audibly, and that to reject their counsel is to reject God. People should beware when their fallible leader says to them, "God has told me. . . ," unless Scripture conclusively declares it. In that case God has not merely told the leader, he has told us all.

For example, a popular, highly respected pastor with great charisma and long tenure was sitting in a church board meeting where a momentous decision was being made. The pastor's proposal involved spending significant sums of money. Some good financial experts on the board advised against what the pastor wanted to do, and the pastor's proposal seemed to be in trouble. While the discussion progressed, the pastor went into his study. After fifteen minutes or so, he came out with tears in his eyes and said, "I've just had a meeting with God and he has told me what we must do!" Obviously, what God told him was what the pastor wanted to do all along. The laymen present were put into a position of having to reject both the pastor's proposal and the will of God (as defined by the pastor whom they loved and respected). It is difficult for the laity to deny the validity of such an experience claimed by a highly respected pastor.

Admittedly, this is an extreme example used to make the point. Most spiritual leaders would never dream of doing such a thing. Yet, in many ways, spiritual leaders may do precisely the same thing, but not always with a clear realization of what they are doing. It is easy for spiritual leaders to insinuate divine support for their plans, thus putting people in an untenable position. Pastors are using highly questionable tactics when they use the pulpit to mix the authoritative Word of God and their personal ideas about church decisions. Thus, without overtly claiming divine sanction, they are putting the imprimatur of God upon their personal preferences, making it difficult for people to differentiate between God's Word and their pastor's opinion. Similarly, a trustee board chairman who claims, "God will be displeased if we budget church finances for this project" is aligning God with his opinion. How does he know that God will be displeased? Rather, the chairman ought to say, "It is my opinion that we should not budget for this project, and these are my reasons for this opinion. . . ."

The appeal to direct revelation must be seen for what it normally is: a pressure tactic to coerce conformity to personal opinion or to the will of God as perceived by a fallible leader. As such, it is unethical.

Of course, someone might object: What if the leader really does have a meeting with God and God tells him what to do? What if he really does know the will of God through direct revelation (that is, not through scriptural revelation)? That remains a possibility; the pastor truly may be another Moses (if your theology allows for that), but when that "revelation" comes to buttress the leader's previously announced position that is in trouble, the probability is that the leader is deceived or is deceiving. At any rate, leaders must scrutinize their own motives and be relentlessly honest with themselves and their followers. God should not be used as a wedge to force conformity.

Cajolery

Persuasion is an honorable art, used by Paul (2 Cor. 5:11) and all spiritual leaders worth their salt. Yet, we must recognize that some forms of persuasion are questionable. Cajolery is persuasion by persistent coaxing, often by flattery or promises. The word comes from a French word (*cajoler*) which means to chatter like a jaybird. The word is used here in its broadest possible sense to include all shady methods of clever enticement.

Attempts to influence and persuade people by the use of smooth, flattering, or beguiling words is mere wheedling. It is coaxing, manipulation for a desired end by adroit handling, cleverness, studied eloquence, or dogged effort. It is this kind of tactic that Paul specifically rejected in his preaching:

> When I came to you, brothers, I did not come with eloquence or superior wisdom as I proclaimed to you the testimony about God. For I resolved to know nothing while I was with you except Jesus Christ and him crucified. I came to you in weakness and fear, and with much trembling. My message and my preaching were not with wise and persuasive words, but with a demonstration of the Spirit's

power, so that your faith might not rest on men's wisdom, but on God's power. [1 Cor. 2:1–5]

And again:

We have renounced secret and shameful ways; we do not use deception, nor do we distort the word of God. On the contrary, by setting forth the truth plainly we commend ourselves to every man's conscience in the sight of God. [2 Cor. 4:2]

Cajolery is simply a form of coerciveness that is subtle, wily, and shrewd. It is the eliciting of a desired response by cleverness, cunning, and chicanery. In reality, it is subterfuge and, hence, not an acceptable motivational technique for spiritual leaders.

Persuasion that avoids cajolery is founded on facts, sound reasoning, logic, common sense, and sincere emotion. All forms of artifice, crafty device, and base deception, however subtle and however effective, must be avoided.

Gimmickry

It is difficult to find a word to describe this category of unworthy behavior. Gimmickry seems to be best, although it really is a slang word that can be used to describe any tricky means of conduct. The word is used to describe the deceptive activity of a magician or carnival pitchman.

Bookstores are filled with "how to gain power over people" books. Some of them have blatantly manipulative titles and philosophies, such as H. W. Gabriel's *Twenty Steps to Power, Influence and Control Over People*. The most popular and convincing book of this kind has been Dale Carnegie's *How to Win Friends and Influence People*, which has gone through more than one hundred printings and has sold more than ten million copies. At last count, it has been translated into twenty-eight languages, and it has been a best seller in all of them.

Such books are filled with practical advice about salesmen's tricks of the trade:

how to get the foot in the door

how to disarm the potential customer

how to answer objections

how to persuade someone against his will

how to beat the competition

how to gain power over people

how to intimidate and win

Anybody (theoretically) can do these things by remembering first names, showing deference, massaging people's self-esteem, admiring their children or home or dog, satisfying basic needs, or arousing fundamental wants. On and on the books go. The suggestion is that if you can master all of these clever strategies, you can get people to do anything you want them to do.

Sometimes spiritual leaders buy into all of this gimmickry and fail to understand that most of it is, after all, another way to coerce people.

> When you have real personal power it hypnotizes others . . . it makes them center on you, makes them feel something of themselves is attached to you, and makes them enjoyably feel you as important to them. That is the personal power you want. You are bored with all the tomfoolery about putting yourself on a common ground with others. You want others to strive for footing on what is your own ground. And you are weary of all the nonsense about needing to establish a bond with others—you want them to try to establish a bond with you!

> Decision making is making your thinking win. . . . When another has put forth thinking that is other than you want it to be, turn his words around for him so they are able to say for him what you want him to say.[3]

This is not true leadership, and most certainly it is not Christian, spiritual servant-leadership. Such gimmickry flows from a low view of humanity. Robert D. Dale is right:

> If I have a low estimate of humanity, I'll tend to rule with an iron hand. Why not? These dolts need all the help they can get! If, on the other hand, I see people as basically gifted and willing to exercise their ministries through the church, I'll tend to give them support and latitude. My leader style grows out of my estimate of human

3. H. W. Gabriel, *Twenty Steps to Power, Influence and Control Over People* (Englewood Cliffs, N.J.: Prentice-Hall, 1962), 3, 142.

nature. In fact, my leader style is the most direct ministry application of my doctrine of humanity.[4]

We close our case with this penetrating insight of James Burns:

> The main failure of these [how-to-gain-power] manuals is more
> pernicious. While few of them today emulate the master in offering
> Machiavellian advice on how to coerce, control, or deceive other
> persons, many do seek to train persons to manage and manipulate
> other persons rather than to *lead* them. The technique is usually that
> of the marketplace manipulation: to play on low-order wants and
> needs and to create hopes and aspirations where none existed be-
> fore, through the use of saturation promotion and propaganda. Worse,
> the manuals treat persons as *things,* as tools to be used or objects
> to be stormed like a castle. At best they search for the lowest com-
> mon denominator of motives among persons and within persons
> and exploit those motives for the benefit of the power wielder, not
> the target.[5]

Worthy Motivational Techniques

If all of the preceding tactics, and others, are manipulative and
unethical, what can leaders do to stimulate decisions that will bring
about change in the structures, forms, methods, and programs of
the church? This question strikes at the very heart of the leaders'
responsibilities.

The responsibility of leaders is to listen, to build teamwork, to
inspire by personal demonstration, to focus on values, and to balance priorities. Leaders model, teach, and guide as they carry out
their tasks. All of these objectives underlie what good, spiritual
leaders do in terms of motivational strategies. Above all, leaders
have a profound respect for the personhood and value of people.
Real leaders do not demean people, belittle their contribution, ignore their problems, or play favorites with people in an effort to
get something accomplished. Spiritual guides are not insensitive
to others' hurts, nor do they run roughshod over the desires of
others. People are not objects, nor are they the means to achieving
a leader's end; they are of inherent worth.

Servant-leaders are extremely sensitive to what is genuinely

4. Robert D. Dale, *Ministers as Leaders* (Nashville: Broadman, 1984), 38.
5. James Burns, *Leadership* (New York: Harper and Row, 1979), 446.

helpful to people in terms of their needs and in terms of biblical injunctions. Leaders set out to help people respect fairness, equity, honesty, responsibility, and justice, and other biblical mandates for living in the social community of the church. Whatever does not contribute to this goal, whatever makes church members dependent upon leaders, whatever fails to respect others' personal identity and self-esteem, should be rejected by spiritual leaders.

The following motivational techniques are regarded as worthy of servant-leaders. Spiritual servant-leaders believe they are also effective, particularly in the long run.

Motivation by Encouragement

Few techniques are as necessary or as fundamental to good motivational leadership as encouragement. Real leaders are always encouraging; they are constantly offering a word of appreciation, writing thank-you notes, cheering on one who stumbles, picking up the bruised, and mending the shattered egos of those who have failed. Spiritual leaders do not miss opportunities to inspire, hearten, elevate, and brighten. "Be of good cheer" are solid, biblical words that every leader can take to heart.

Imagine a father sitting in the stands watching his son play football. Suppose he were to yell, "You idiot! You dummy! You blew it again! You are a very poor player! Why don't you quit?" None of us can imagine that such tactics would motivate the boy to play better football. Such words would most likely prompt him to quit. Yet, Sunday after Sunday the gist of many sermons is, "Shape up, folks! You're not cutting it! You're worse than any of us imagine!" Rebuke, and that of a harsh kind, has often usurped the place of encouragement. If it receives this kind of verbal abuse and battering from it leaders, it is a wonder that the church ever is motivated to achieve anything significant for God.

The ministry of encouragement by the early leaders of the church, so prominent in the New Testament, ought to guide us in our own motivational efforts. Witness this small sampling of dozens of such texts:

> Judas and Silas, who themselves were prophets, said much to encourage and strengthen the brothers. [Acts 15:32]

> I am sending [Tychicus] to you for this very purpose, that you may know how we are, and that he may encourage you. [Eph. 6:22]

For you know that we dealt with each of you as a father deals with his own children, encouraging, comforting and urging you to live lives worthy of God, who calls you into his kingdom and glory. [1 Thess. 2:11–12]

Other pertinent texts are Colossians 4:8; 1 Thessalonians 3:2; 4:18; 5:11, 14; 2 Timothy 4:2; Titus 1:9; 2:6, 15; Hebrews 3:13; 10:25. Indeed, it seems as though the primary motivational strategy of God is his encouragement of us: "May our Lord Jesus Christ himself and God our Father, who loved us and by his grace gave us eternal encouragement and good hope, encourage your hearts and strengthen you in every good deed and word" (2 Thess. 2:16–17). The word of encouragement is always appropriate, and it is one of the most powerful tools in the spiritual leader's strategy for effecting change. It is not only powerful, but also proper and necessary.

It is true that sometimes leaders must also give a word of rebuke, as did Paul on some occasions. Even then, the rebuke must be encouraging, not merely censuring or scolding. Sometimes church leaders vent their own frustration and reveal their own hostility rather than cheer the church on to greater achievement.

Motivation Through Qualitative Ministry

Spiritual leaders in the church are primarily responsible for the ministry of the Word of God and for prayer. It undoubtedly has been the intention of God from the beginning that people should be moved and motivated to change by the inner conviction of the Holy Spirit in response to the declaration of his Word and in response to intercessory prayer. The early apostles desired others to assume certain tasks so that they would not neglect the ministry of the word of God: "We will turn this responsibility over to them and will give our attention to prayer and the ministry of the word" (Acts 6:3–4).

How much more effective could spiritual leaders be if they spent half as much time trying to maneuver people politically and twice as much time in prayer and preparation for the ministry of the Word so that people might be moved to action by the Holy Spirit. Kenneth O. Gangel emphasized this: "The leaders in the local church, on the other hand, are able to depend upon and, indeed, bring to bear a supernatural force which changes human behavior from the inside out rather than from the outside in."[6]

Care must be taken here, because even the Word of God can be used deceitfully and for selfish purposes. Leaders sometimes use preaching, proof-texting, pious languge, and scholarly insights to gain unfair advantage in promoting their own agenda. All of this is a distortion of the sacred responsibility of one who "correctly handles the word of truth" (2 Tim. 2:15).

The patient, consistent proclamation of scriptural truth and competent spiritual direction, coupled with serious intercessory prayer, brings the power of the Holy Spirit to bear on any situation. Decisions are made and change is prompted in such churches, not by the power of dynamic, charismatic personalities, or by questionable methods, but by the quiet, sometimes slow, certain conviction of God's people who are brought to live under the mandate of the Word of God.

The pastoral search committee of a large Midwestern church was interviewing a candidate for senior pastor. The church had had a particularly distasteful experience with its previous pastor, who had advocated a building program that people felt was unnecessary. The candidate was asked, "Would you push our church to enter a building program?" The candidate, although he was unaware of the experience of the church with the former pastor, answered, "No. I believe that my responsibility is to preach, teach, and shepherd the church. If God should so bless that ministry with much fruit, the church would have a problem of physical growth, and I would expect the spiritual leadership and the church to face and handle that problem wisely." In a few short years the church was involved in a major building program, not because the pastor urged it, but because his ministry was truly effective. The motivation to build arose from within the people, who looked at how God was blessing and said, "We've got to do something."

Today's most effective churches are led by leaders who major not in pulling strings, but in ministering effectively. Growth and all of the decisions that growth necessitates are motivated and produced in such churches not by political power play or various

6. Kenneth O. Gangel, *Building Leaders for Church Education* (Chicago: Moody, 1981), 367.

questionable tactics, but by excellence in spiritual ministries. Such excellence is ethical, powerful, and unifying.

Motivation by Entrusting Responsibility

It is morally right to involve people in decisions that affect them. To treat people like dolts is insulting to rational adults and counterproductive to group motivation. Therefore, good leaders involve people in the process of decision making whenever those decisions affect their lives. Tremendous motivational power is brought to bear upon people who are believed in, entrusted with responsibility, and summoned to participate in shaping the future.

People are seldom properly motivated when they are excluded from the process. Good leaders know that the more people are involved in group thinking and pooling their talents and energies, the more they are motivated to achieve worthwhile objectives: "Good group thinking is a process that leads to reliable and convincing group decision, just as good individual thinking is a process that leads to reliable and convincing individual decision."[7]

This means, among other things, that leaders are not afraid of conflict. As a matter of fact, leaders stimulate healthy conflict, believing that better decisions come from the free exchange of conflicting opinions. It is noteworthy that when the early church had to make a difficult decision, it allowed for a heated debate: "This brought Paul and Barnabas into sharp dispute and debate (Greek *suzētēsis*) with them. . . . After much discussion (*suzētēsis*), Peter got up and addressed them . . ." (Acts 15:2, 7). The debate was a good thing; a better decision came out of it. This is examined in greater detail in chapter 12.

Open expression by people who differ is not threatening to a good leader; it is positive and necessary to the formation of consensus. Good leaders want all the relevant facts and opinions out so that decisions are made by the group acting in concert, for "the degree of consensus reached by members and subgroups often determines the degree to which the organization can accomplish its purposes effectively."[8]

Also, mustering church resources and entrusting people with

7. Grace Elliott, *How to Help Groups Make Decisions* (New York: Association, 1959), 12.

8. David O. Moberg, *The Church as a Social Institution* (Grand Rapids: Baker, 1984), 241.

responsibility means that leaders are always process persons, conscious of how things are done. They are not afraid to postpone a decision so that new opinions can be solicited or additional facts uncovered. Time is not the crucial dimension except in an emergency; rather, the best possible decision and the unity of the church are paramount. Good leaders seldom yield to the urgency of the moment, unless there really is an emergency, which is rare in church life.

Trusting people and deploying resources mean that leaders motivate by involving people, giving them responsibility, helping them to define the issues, clarifying the possibilities and the choices, recognizing the reasons behind actions, emphasizing points of agreement, exploring areas of differences, and moving the discussion toward integration of facts and opinions. The result of such tactics at the great Jerusalem council was that "[w]hen decisions were made they were made by the whole company of believers, not simply the officials."[9]

Good spiritual leaders are firmly convinced that such motivational tactics are ethical, elevating, and effective. They respect human dignity, they distinguish honorable leadership, and they produce better decisions in the church for healthy change.

The Ethical Use of Emotion

A special word must be said about the use of emotion in leadership. Few things are as powerful as emotion. It is difficult but imperative that leaders use emotion ethically. One does not have to be around a church for long to observe the sheer power of an emotional appeal exerted by the use of supercharged words (e.g., desecration, diabolical, or monstrous) or red-faced anger or tears. Demonstrations of emotion can easily neutralize reason and overwhelm facts. Both leaders and followers can be guilty of the misuse of emotion. Leaders can misuse emotion to effect the submission of followers, and followers can misuse emotion to justify rebellion against leaders.

Sincere emotion is not unethical. The best leaders use emotion, but always judiciously and never excessively. Biblical leaders fre-

9. Donald Guthrie, *New Testament Theology* (Downers Grove: Inter-Varsity, 1981), 741.

quently used strong emotion in influencing people and decisions. For example, Peter's speech at the Jerusalem council contained these words: "Now then, why do you try to test God by putting on the necks of the disciples a yoke that neither we nor our fathers have been able to bear? No! We believe it is through the grace of our Lord Jesus that we are saved, just as they are" (Acts 15:10–11). Peter's words were powerful because of their obvious emotion (as well as logic). Moses was demonstrably emotional on more than one occasion when circumstances warranted it. Christ was emotional in weeping over Jerusalem, in cleansing the temple, and in his severe judgment of the hypocrites (Matt. 23). Paul wept as he attempted to influence people; his letters often contained strong, emotional language: "For I wrote you out of great distress and anguish of heart and with many tears, not to grieve you but to let you know the depth of my love for you" (2 Cor. 2:4).

Certainly we cannot reject the use of emotion and passion in preaching or in sharing personal convictions. Emotion is an integral part of motivation, zeal, sincerity, and inspiration. J. Oswald Sanders wrote, "Great leaders who have turned the tide in days of national and spiritual declension have been men who could get angry at the injustices and abuses which dishonor God and enslave men."[10]

Sometimes church leaders are afraid of emotion. The fear of emotion has caused emotion to be downgraded in importance and ridiculed as an acceptable persuasive tool by some people. Preachers ought to know how important emotion is in their preaching. Our fear of emotion must not cripple our leadership. John R. W. Stott sounds the correct note: "We should not fear genuine emotion. . . . More to be feared than emotion is cold professionalism, the dry, detached utterance of a lecture which has neither heart nor soul in it."[11] At least some of us will agree with Charles Spurgeon, who proclaimed, "Even fanaticism is to be preferred to indifference. I had sooner risk the dangers of a tornado of religious excitement than see the air grow stagnant with a dead formality."[12] Healthy, honest, controlled emotion is worthy of the best of leaders.

Yet, emotion can easily become a manipulative device and

10. J. Oswald Sanders, *Spiritual Leadership* (Chicago: Moody, 1967), 61.

11. John R. W. Stott, *The Preacher's Portrait* (Grand Rapids: Eerdmans, 1961), 58.

12. Charles Spurgeon, *All-Round Ministry* (reprint ed.; Carlisle, Penn.: Banner of Truth, 1972), 173.

unethical. What guidelines can be suggested for the ethical use of emotion in the leadership of the church? The following are offered for consideration.

Emotion Must Not Substitute for Rationality

Emotion may be used as a buttress to reason, but never as a substitute for reason. If emotional display is used to gain acceptance of an unworthy, irrational argument or concept, emotion is misused.

Some leaders are too intellectually lazy to do the tedious work of sound reasoning and digging for facts, preferring instead to depend on strong emotion turned on at the appropriate moment. If a leader believes a situation justifies an aggressive attempt to influence opinion, that leader should have logical, intelligent facts and a carefully reasoned argument to present. Logical reasoning may be supported by the emotion of earnest sincerity and conviction, but no emotion can be allowed which is a substitute for sound thinking. Leaders who use emotion to cover up a deficiency in rationality behave unethically.

Emotion Must Be Honest

Permissible emotion must always be genuine. Emotional displays that are put on constitute hoaxes. People generally react negatively if they suspect that a leader "turns on the tears at will." Conjuring up emotional display to gain personal advantage or to arouse sympathy is reprehensible. Integrity demands a rigorous honesty in the use of emotion. Emotion is not honest if it becomes a tool that the leader uses with premeditated shrewdness to achieve a desired end.

When Jesus cleansed the temple, he was righteously indignant; he didn't merely sound angry, he was angry. When Moses lashed out at the people for erecting a golden calf, he really was angry; it was not merely a performance or display. When Paul expressed joyful appreciation to the Philippians, he really felt that way; his joy was not conjured up to achieve a desired effect.

Emotion Must Not Manipulate

Manipulation is not always easy to identify, and people differ on what constitutes exploitative emotion. However, some of the tactics of manipulation seem obvious: flattery, threat, favoritism, begging, cajolery, proof-texting, bribery, appeals to direct revelation, and flaunting expertise. Emotion is unethical when used to buttress such methods so that leaders can get their way. Most conscientious church leaders reject such tactics of emotional display, and most church members recognize such theatrics more quickly than leaders imagine.

Admittedly, this is a fine line, and each person may draw the line in a slightly different place according to conscience. If congregations once become convinced that they are being manipulated by emotional appeal, it is unlikely that the leaders will exercise any healthy influence. It is also likely that such leaders will be ultimately rejected by their constituents.

Emotion Must Not Become Emotionalism

Emotionalism is differentiated from healthy emotion by a matter of degrees. Emotionalism is excessive appeal to the emotions, a display of undue, uncontrolled, or unwarranted emotion.

Emotionalism is relative and subjective, and people will differ on what they consider excessive. Nevertheless, people are quick to recognize the difference between righteous indignation and a temper tantrum. People know the difference between genuine tears of sympathy and uncontrolled hysteria or wailing. Earnest expression of sentiment is necessary and acceptable; irrational display and histrionics are not.

Leaders must constantly scrutinize their attitudes and methodology to see if their emotional behavior is unethical or is perceived to be unethical. This necessitates a keen spiritual sensitivity.

Summary

Leadership effectiveness depends upon the ability of leaders to stimulate followers to make decisions and take action. Motivational techniques can easily become unethical and manipulative.

Spiritual leaders must guard against motivational pragmatism, an end-justifies-means philosophy. Any technique that is basically coercive is unethical, unbiblical, and unworthy of Christian leaders. Not only the obvious tactics such as lying, threat, and bribery are unethical, but also appeals to direct revelation, cajolery, and gimmickry of all sorts are inappropriate tactics for spiritual leaders.

Ethical techniques for spiritual leaders include motivation by encouragement, by qualitative ministry, and by involving people, all techniques founded on a respect for people and their hopes, dreams, problems, hurts, and inherent worth.

The ethical use of emotion is a serious problem in the church. The use of proper emotion is not only good, but necessary. However, emotion must not be used as a substitute for rationality; emotion must not be dishonest; emotion must not be used as a manipulative tactic; and emotion must not be allowed to degenerate into immoderate display of theatrics.

12

Leadership in Decision Making
A Case Study

There is little that is prescriptive in the New Testament about church decision making. Nowhere are we given a systematic treatment of how God intends churches to make decisions and bring about change. God apparently saw fit to leave decision making to the prayerful discernment of individual churches under the guidance of the Holy Spirit and spiritual leaders. Scripture concentrates on the spiritual qualifications of leaders, and specific leadership behavior is left to wisdom and the application of broad scriptural principles.

Despite the absence of prescriptive direction for decision making, Acts 15 gives an excellent description of how the early church came to a decision on a divisive issue. Church leaders are wise to examine this sacred record for insight on how both leaders and churches should behave in the process of achieving consensus on thorny issues.

The account in Acts 15 is not prescriptive, nor is it given in great

185

detail. Nevertheless, it is a good model, and some might even consider it normative. Extraordinary wisdom and spiritual insight were demonstrated in achieving a satisfactory decision on an issue that had the potential to divide Christendom into two permanent factions, one of Jewish believers and one of Gentile believers. If today's church leaders would follow the principles of decision making revealed in Acts 15, the church may be more disposed to maintain harmony, make wise decisions, and prosper spiritually.

The early church survived and grew dramatically in a hostile environment and came to an acceptable decision on a delicate, sensitive issue with a broad consensus and obvious satisfaction. There is reason to believe that the same methodology of decision making that served the infant church so well would serve us equally effectively.

It is not our purpose here to give an exhaustive exposition of Acts 15, but merely to note the basic principles of behavior exhibited by the early church. Excellent biblical scholars have dealt adequately with the historical, literary, theological, and grammatical difficulties in the passage. The serious student of the text should read F. F. Bruce's *Acts of the Apostles* and other exegetical commentaries.

It is surprising and disappointing that few authors have examined this significant event in the life of the early church from the standpoint of leadership behavior and church decision making. Scholars have been far more concerned with technical matters of textual exposition, historical significance, cultural understanding, and critical analysis. More attention needs to be given to the process of church decision making as revealed in this passage. Perhaps the absence of many details has discouraged the church from considering the decision-making methods of the early leaders.

The Problem

It is difficult, perhaps impossible, for most of us in our culture to appreciate the magnitude of the problem precipitated in the early church by the conversion of Gentiles to belief in Jesus as Messiah, Savior, and Lord. The first Jewish believers in Christ undoubtedly considered themselves the faithful remnant of Israel. However, Gentiles were beginning to confess Christ in numbers that threatened the church's understanding of itself. Were Gentile believers to be incorporated into one body with Jewish believers? If so, under what conditions? Were Gentile believers to be circumcised and required to obey the ceremonial laws of Moses that were so precious to the Jews, just as Jewish proselytes were expected to do?

The lucid and definitive revelation given to Paul concerning this matter had not yet been made clear to the church at large, nor even to some of the leaders in the early church. No authoritative biblical texts like the following could be cited at that time.

> In reading this, then, you will be able to understand my insight into the mystery of Christ, which was not made known to men in other generations as it has now been revealed by the Spirit to God's holy apostles and prophets. This mystery is that through the gospel the Gentiles are heirs together with Israel, members together of one body, and sharers together in the promise in Christ Jesus. [Eph. 3:4–6]

and

> For in Christ Jesus neither circumcision nor uncircumcision has any value. [Gal. 5:6]

and

> A man is not a Jew if he is only one outwardly, nor is circumcision merely outward and physical. No, a man is a Jew if he is one inwardly; and circumcision is circumcision of the heart, by the Spirit, not by the written code. Such a man's praise is not from men, but from God. [Rom. 2:28–29]

If the Gentile believers were to be accepted into one body with Jewish believers, under what conditions? The issue was extraordinarily complex, yet at its core it had a simple, crucial dimension involving the fundamental conception of the grace of God. Luke T. Johnson states the problem concisely:

> By challenging the Antioch community at the level of its own salvation, the Judeans put the question in its starkest terms: is the grace of God and the gift of the Holy Spirit sufficient for salvation, or not? And this touches another question: is God's work going to

be acknowledged as it manifests itself, or only as it conforms to the church's presuppositions?[1]

The issue, which had undoubtedly been brewing for some years, was brought to a head by some men who came to Antioch from Judea. They began to teach, "Unless you are circumcised, according to the custom taught by Moses, you cannot be saved" (Acts 15:1). At Jerusalem, the issue was articulated in more detail and seemed to include full obedience to the law of Moses: "Then some of the believers who belonged to the party of the Pharisees stood up and said, 'The Gentiles must be circumcised and required to obey the law of Moses' " (Acts 15:5).

This doctrine was heresy to Paul and Barnabas, who obviously believed in a purer form of God's grace in the salvation of the Gentiles and Jews alike. In Jerusalem, Peter expressed the conviction of Paul and Barnabas: "No! We believe it is through the grace of our Lord Jesus that [Jews] are saved, just as [Gentiles] are" (Acts 15:11).

Paul later expressed his doctrinal creed: "But now a righteousness from God, apart from law, has been made known, to which the Law and the Prophets testify. This righteousness from God comes through faith in Jesus Christ to all who believe" (Rom. 3:21). The suggestion by the Judeans that the Gentiles could not be saved without the rite of circumcision "brought Paul and Barnabas into sharp dispute and debate with them" (Acts 15:2).

The Greek words (*stasis*, dissension; *suzētēsis*, disputation) used in verse 2 reveal the seriousness of the argument. The word *stasis* is the same word variously translated "insurrection" (Mark 15:7), "sedition" (Luke 23:19, 25), and "uproar" (Acts 19:40 KJV). The biblical account indicates that "Paul and Barnabas had a fierce argument and dispute with them about this" (Acts 15:2 TEV).

It is clear that there was a lengthy and heated debate both at Antioch and later at Jerusalem over this issue. The differences in basic understanding about salvation doctrine were sharp. There was grave danger of polarizing the church, some following the teaching of Paul and Barnabas and others following those legalists who belonged to the sect of the Pharisees.

The point in question was a policy-making issue; feelings ran

---

1. Luke T. Johnson, *Decision Making in the Chruch* (Philadelphia: Fortress, 1983), 78.

deep. The problem struck at the most sensitive value systems of the Jewish people, for the law of Moses was not to be dismissed lightly. The division threatened the unity of the church and jeopardized the teaching of Paul, who stated, even at this rather early stage of his ministry, "that a man is justified by faith apart from observing the law. Is God the God of Jews only? Is he not the God of Gentiles too? Yes, of Gentiles too, since there is only one God, who will justify the circumcised by faith and the uncircumcised through that same faith" (Rom. 3:28–30).

Such a divisive issue could not long go unresolved. The question needed to be resolved in a way that would maintain the unity and basic harmony of the fledgling church, but not contaminate the doctrine of salvation by grace alone, "apart from observing the law."

The Church at Antioch

A great dispute erupted in Antioch when some men from Judea taught the necessity of circumcision for Gentile converts. Paul and Barnabas took issue with such teaching. The dissension became such that the Christians at Antioch felt that they could not resolve it. How the church at Antioch reached the conclusion that it could not resolve the dilemma is not revealed. It seems safe to conclude that even after much debate no consensus could be reached.

Therefore, appeal was made to the mother church at Jerusalem. The leaders there, esteemed apostles and elders, were respected and trusted for their spiritual maturity on doctrinal matters. "So Paul and Barnabas were appointed, along with some other believers, to go up to see the apostles and elders about this question" (Acts 15:2). It would be interesting to know if the Antioch church was optimistic that the decision would be satisfactory to the various factions. Apparently, however, the Christians at Antioch were determined to abide by whatever decision came from Jerusalem.

Perhaps the first lesson to be learned from this account is that there are times when discretionary wisdom calls for wider, more mature spiritual counsel than is immediately available. There existed in the early church a respect for the elders and apostles, a respect that compelled the church to seek their wisdom and submit to their judgment. It seems rare in our day to find this spirit of respect and deference to wise leaders inside or outside of the local church. Perhaps a lack of wise spiritual leaders contributes to the problem.

Proponents of certain church structures see in this account justification for authoritarian control by denominational leaders. However, in the light of the entire passage, this seems unwarranted. The final words of the letter sent to Antioch were, "You will do well to avoid these things" (Acts 15:29). Such an exhortation represents an irenic spirit and reveals a respect for the church at Antioch. The decision rendered was couched in language carefully calculated to be gentle and gracious, not insistent and autocratic: "It seemed good to the Holy Spirit and to us" (Acts 15:28). The message sent from Jerusalem was not merely a little piece of calculated advice, but neither was it a totalitarian dictum. It was spiritual guidance, and it was received by those desiring such guidance.

The decision articulated by James and confirmed by the whole church was not an order issued by one man, but an expression of the wisdom and spiritual discernment of the Jerusalem church. There is no evidence to suggest that the believers in Antioch felt that conformity was being demanded of them; rather, they "were glad for [the] encouraging message" (Acts 15:31). The indication is that the church did not feel that it was commanded to submit to a decree; rather, the church felt encouraged, and the people joyfully recognized and deferred to the wisdom of the Jerusalem church. We are left to wonder what would have happened if the church at Antioch had rejected the counsel from Jerusalem.

The Meetings at Jerusalem

Exactly what happened when the commissioned group arrived in Jerusalem is unclear. The indication is that multiple meetings were held. Four verses give insight to what went on, but they are far from definitive and leave many questions. First, there was an initial meeting: "When they came to Jerusalem, they [the group from Antioch] were welcomed by the church and the apostles and elders, to whom they reported everything God had done through them" (Acts 15:4).

This verse suggests that there was an open meeting of the church (Greek *ekklēsia*), under the direction of the apostles and elders, at which the group from Antioch gave a report of its ministry. We do not know how large the church at Jerusalem was at this time. Probably there were numerous house-churches in the city that met from week to week as was customary in early church history, but the indication is that on this occasion there was a larger meeting, and the Jerusalem assembly was referred to as "the church," meaning those believers who were present.

Second, there is reference to a meeting of the apostles and elders: "The apostles and elders met to consider this question" (Acts 15:6). When this verse is isolated from the whole context it appears that this meeting was exclusively for apostles and elders, and we are not told how many apostles and elders there were. However, in the light of what follows, it seems unlikely that this was a closed meeting. Therefore, this particular verse merely means that the meeting was called by and presided over by the apostles and elders. Verse 6 must be interpreted in the light of verses 12 and 22, which refer to the "whole assembly" and the "whole church." In any case, the representatives from Antioch were present, in addition to the Jerusalem apostles and elders.

Third, there is a reference to a large gathering of believers: "The whole assembly became silent as they listened to Barnabas and Paul telling about the miraculous signs and wonders God had done among the Gentiles through them" (Acts 15:12). The Greek word for "assembly" (*plēthos*) in this verse is frequently translated "multitude" or "a great company" (e.g., "a great company of the heavenly host" [Luke 2:13]) or "a large number" (e.g., "the large number of fish" [John 21:6]). The New International Version translates this Greek word "the church" in Acts 15:30. The use of the word *plēthos* at least implies that a substantially larger group was present, not just a select group of apostles and elders. It seems reasonable to suggest that other members of both the Jerusalem and Antioch churches were present and participated in the debate.

Fourth, there is a definite reference to the whole church: "Then the apostles and elders, with the whole church, decided to choose some of their own men and send them to Antioch with Paul and Barnabas" (Acts 15:22). In this verse the Greek word is *ekklēsia*, the customary word used when referring to the church as a corporate body. It is preceded by the words *the whole* as if to emphasize that the decision was not one of the elders and apostles, but one in which the whole church participated. Of course, it is possible that the meeting referred to in verse 22 was subsequent to the meeting in which the primary decision was articulated by James. Scripture is not definitive on this point, and we are left to make reasonable inferences. However this is interpreted, it certainly is obvious that the whole church concurred with the decision articulated by James.

It seems reasonable to suggest that more than one meeting was held, perhaps many over the course of some weeks. The issue was so difficult and divisive that in all probability the early Christians spent much time in prayer about it, although the text does not say specifically that they did. Knowing something about the early church and its habits of prayer (see Acts 2:42; 12:12), it is impossible to believe that the Christians did not pray much about this difficult decision. Certainly the letter sent to Antioch indicates that the decision bore the imprint of the Holy Spirit: "It seemed good to the Holy Spirit and to us" (Acts 15:28). The church was confident of the Spirit's guidance. Could they have been so confident had they not prayed much?

Further, there seems little doubt that the leaders examined the Old Testament records for indications of God's will in the matter, something difficult to do in a short public meeting. James infers that the excerpt from Amos (Acts 15:16–18) is only representative of what other Old Testament prophets taught, for he introduces the text by saying, "The words of the prophets are in agreement" (Acts 15:15).

If we can consider the procedure of the early church a good model, these conclusions apply to the modern church:

1. Major policy decisions affecting the whole church should be made by open discussion with all interested parties. Leaders should preside over such meetings, participate in the debate, allow dissent, attempt to influence by logic, facts, and sincere emotion, and generally guide the church to a decision. They should avoid highhanded methodology: limiting debate or making unilateral decisions on controversial, emotionally supercharged issues. Leaders must allow time for consensus to form.

2. The church should spend considerable time in prayer about its major decisions, seeking the direction and blessing of God. Churches are greatly enriched when they can sincerely say, "It seemed good to the Holy Spirit and to us."

3. All relevant Scripture should be examined for clues to what God's desire might be. The task of bringing Scripture to bear upon an issue is a primary responsibility of church elders who should have superior training in biblical understanding. While Scripture does not give a mandate for all controversial decisions, there usually are applicable principles.

The Great Debate

Whatever the text suggests about the number of meetings and the people who were present, the passage makes it clear that a great, heated debate took place, a debate at which anyone present could speak his mind. The words *much discussion* (Acts 15:7) indicate that the issue was not decided in a short time. It would be interesting to know exactly how long the discussion went on: hours . . . or days . . . or weeks?

Of course, there is no way to be certain, but it seems unlikely that so thorny an issue was decided in one meeting, whatever its length. The complexity of the problem and the passion of the interested parties demanded much discussion which probably prompted leaders to search the Scriptures and call for times of prayer, after which the church met again for more discussion.

The leaders encouraged participation of the group, and the debate revealed much conflict:

> The larger assembly is still present and the discussion takes place before them (cf. 15:12, 22), but the leaders now actively articulate the question. After that initial sharp clash of views, there follows a great debate (15:7). For a writer of marked irenic tendencies, Luke exposes much conflict in this narrative.[2]

The apostles and elders considered it their responsibility to see that the decision was acceptable to the wider body, rather than to just a handful of leaders. Leaders thought it their responsibility to allow for and encourage the free, open sharing of opinions, convictions, and insights. There is no indication in the text that leaders grabbed for power, usurped control over the church, took unilateral action, or made decisions behind closed doors without the participation and consent of the church. The lesson for the modern church

2. Ibid., 80.

is that when there is an issue of major consequence that affects the church body, the wisdom and discernment of the whole group is needed. Individuals and small groups may do research and bring their findings to the larger group's attention, but they should not deny free expression of other opinions.

There is no hint in the text that the debate was limited, as frequently happens in the modern church, dedicated as it is to proper parliamentary procedure and the conservation of time. Scripture has a way of compressing events, almost making them sound as though they happened in a short time. It is far more likely, however, that so controversial an issue called for multiple meetings with unlimited discussion by all who wished to participate, until finally a consensus evolved in the church.

It is particularly noteworthy that after much discussion Peter "got up and addressed" (Acts 15:7) the multitude. It was not characteristic for Peter to wait while many others spoke. Why was Peter silent for so long? Perhaps he spoke earlier, and his speech was not recorded for us. After Peter made his impassioned plea, Paul and Barnabas told about the miraculous signs and wonders God had done among the Gentiles through them. Why did not Paul and Barnabas do this earlier? James, apparently the presiding elder in the Jerusalem church, did not speak (as far as the record indicates) until Paul and Barnabas finished their story.

Seemingly, these influential people in the church held their tongues while others were allowed to carry on a heated debate. Why? Probably not because they were undecided. Paul sharply disputed with the Judaizers at Antioch and vigorously defended freedom in Christ Jesus: "This matter arose because some false brothers had infiltrated our ranks to spy on the freedom we have in Christ Jesus and to make us slaves. We did not give in to them for a moment, so that the truth of the gospel might remain with you" (Gal. 2:4–5).

It may be that the influential leaders were silent because they simply desired the participation of all present and realized that if they spoke prematurely and vehemently others might be intimidated. Some may think that this is reading too much into the text; perhaps it is. Certainly it is speculation, but reasonable guesswork.

At any rate, the decision was made in concert with the whole church, with the approval of the whole church, and it was the church that chose Judas and Silas to send word of the agreement to Antioch. Today there is a struggle over so-called elder rule in many churches. The expression is distasteful to many on several counts, not the least of which is the authoritarian implication of the English word *rule*.[3] There is little indication that the early church leaders decreed; rather, they presided over the church and even solicited the participation and wisdom of the wider fellowship of believers in making crucial decisions. However, there are those who vigorously disagree with this interpretation of the events recorded in Acts 15 and devoutly believe that leaders are entrusted with legislative power over the church. All, however, must come to grips with the teaching of Jesus and Peter prohibiting autocracy.

The Consensus

A superficial reading of the text might lead to the conclusion that James made the final decision unilaterally, handed down his edict, and expected the church to yield to it. This does not seem to be the case. Rather, a consensus was formed which James discerned and articulated:

> "It is my judgment, therefore, that we should not make it difficult for the Gentiles who are turning to God. Instead, we should write to them, telling them to abstain from food polluted by idols, from sexual immorality, from the meat of strangled animals and from blood. For Moses has been preached in every city from the earliest times and is read in the synagogues on every Sabbath." [Acts 15:19–21]

The meaning of consensus does not lie in a vote, but in the unity and commitment to a decision after it is made. The proof that consensus was achieved is simply that there was wide acceptance of the decision in the church, although the decision had major ramifications for many people. Even those who had "belonged to the party of the Pharisees" and had urged that "Gentiles must be circumcised and required to obey the law of Moses" apparently held their peace in satisfaction with the decision. The Christians at Antioch "were glad for [the] encouraging message." The issue

3. "Rule: to exercise control over; govern; to dominate by powerful influence; hold sway over; to decide or declare judicially; decree; to exercise authority; be in control or command." *The American Heritage Dictionary*, 2d college ed., 1985.

seemed to be settled. The conclusion of James was a solemn, con-
sensual judgment, one that gained the approval of the assembly
(Acts 15:22, 25). The problem of Judaizers did not immediately go
away, but the church was forever settled on a sound theological
foundation; salvation by grace was upheld, and the church was
given clear direction on an extraordinarily sensitive issue.

The important fact is that a decision emerged out of free, spir-
ited, and unlimited discussion. The consensus probably formed
rapidly at the end of the debate as Peter, Paul, and Barnabas spoke.
B. Aubrey Fisher states what often happens in a situation such as
this:

> The process of emergence is gradual and cumulative. A specific
> point in time at which decisions are made is not apt to be found.
> In fact, the emergence process presupposes that groups achieve con-
> sensus on their decisions *after* those decisions appear to have been
> made. The very final stage of interaction, then, fulfills the purpose
> of procuring members' public commitment, the essence of consen-
> sus, to decisions already reached.[4]

The proof that many modern church decisions are poor ones is
found in the degree of dissatisfaction expressed in the fellowship
after the decisions are made. Churches frequently reformulate decisions which were obviously bad ones in the beginning. The proof
of a poor decision is that it meets with great dissatisfaction among
the constituency. Good leaders work and wait for consensus on
sensitive issues, even if the debate continues through many meetings. Spiritual servant-leaders are not gratified by a slim plurality
of votes. Rarely, if ever, are good leaders satisfied with a simple
majority vote on important issues of policy.

The leaders in Jerusalem did not bring the issue to a premature
vote, nor did they resolve the problem by majority rule. There is
no evidence to suggest that voting of any kind was done, unless
it was in the selection of Judas and Silas to go with Paul and
Barnabas to Antioch, after the primary decision had emerged from
the discussion. The process of discussion in the evolution of a
decision is described by Fisher: "Group decision making, like leadership, possesses no single 'best' or correct answer to be discov-

4. B. Aubrey Fisher, *Small Group Decision Making: Communication and Group Process*
(New York: McGraw-Hill, 1974), 139.

ered in a 'Eureka!' or 'Aha!' manner. It is reasonable to conclude that groups do not *make* decisions. Decisions *emerge* from group interaction."[5]

Consensus does not mean that the decision was identical to what each person would have made unilaterally. Rather, consensus means that there was general agreement that the decision announced by James was the wisest and the best possible one given the circumstances, the facts, and the value systems of the people. People did not go away feeling slighted or that a slim majority had inflicted its will on a sizable minority. It may not have been a decision that pleased everybody perfectly, but it was a decision that the membership of the church could live with, be glad for, and support. The arguments of Judaizers were eventually silenced because the church had spoken definitively and wisely.

Church leaders today should learn from this case study in decision making. Voting may have its place with respect to some issues of lesser consequence, or when time constraints dictate the need for efficiency, but to bring important matters of policy that involve strong emotions and value systems to a precipitate vote, dividing the house, is unwise and potentially explosive. Time must be given for extended debate and for consensus to develop.

Most longstanding church members have been in church business meetings where crucial concerns were being decided. After ten minutes or so someone impatiently shouts, "I move the previous question!" or simply, "Question!" This is a motion to end debate and bring the matter to an immediate vote, in spite of the fact that others may still want to speak on the issue. Moving the previous question is a motion that, according to parliamentary procedure, takes precedence over the discussion on the floor. It must not! Parliamentary procedure has the primary purpose of expediting things; some things must not be expedited if the Spirit of God is to work in the church. The chairman or moderator should calmly rule the motion out of order. The goal is consensus, not quick decision by majority rule. Others have a right to be heard. It may be that few things have so squelched the working of the Spirit of God in church business meetings as has premature voting. It is often better to make no decision than to divide and polarize the body by an impulsive vote to shorten the business meeting.

5. Ibid.

The Compromise

The consensus decision articulated by James was a compromise between the extreme positions of the two sides. The question was, "Should Gentile converts be circumcised and required to obey the law of Moses?" The irenic answer of the church was "It seemed good to the Holy Spirit and to us not to burden you with anything beyond the following requirements: You are to abstain from food sacrificed to idols, from blood, from the meat of strangled animals and from sexual immorality. You will do well to avoid these things" (Acts 15:28–29).

Certain concessions were made to those zealous for the Mosaic law, while the basic principle of salvation by grace through faith was upheld. The rationalization of James for these concessions was, "For Moses has been preached in every city from the earliest times and is read in the synagogues on every Sabbath" (Acts 15:21). The decision did not require circumcision for Gentile converts, but it did make some requirements pertaining both to the moral law and to ceremonial law given by God through Moses. Even these were given with the winsome words, "You will do well to avoid these things" (Acts 15:29).

The purist on matters of grace might object to the ceremonial requirements, as Paul did later in writing to the Corinthians about meat offered to idols. There is no doubt that the overwhelming majority, including Peter, Paul, and Barnabas, regarded the decision an acceptable compromise. They could and did support it.

The proponents of Mosaic law did not get everything they wanted, but they were satisfied that the law was not totally discounted. It was recognized that significant concessions were made. These concessions made possible continued fellowship and the existence of one united body. There was no division, at least partly because of the compromise made.

There was give and take in the process. Seldom can questions of major importance involving value systems be reduced to "Who is right and who is wrong?" Rather, such issues necessitate posing the question, "What is the best possible solution that will not compromise fundamental convictions, but that will preserve the unity of the body?" James was wise and spiritually perceptive to recognize that a compromise position was needed to satisfy the church as a whole. Good church leaders patiently work for an acceptable compromise so that consensus might be achieved.

The decision was a compromise compatible with Scripture, though not specifically dictated by Scripture. No Old Testament proof-text could be cited that specifically addressed the precise issue before the church. The mystery of the church as one body containing Jews and Gentiles "for ages past was kept hidden in God, who created all things" (Eph. 3:9). Yet, numerous passages indicated that in the latter days God would reach out to the Gentiles; James cited one such text. The consensus decision was perfectly compatible with the prophecies and did not "make it difficult for the Gentiles who are turning to God" (Acts 15:19). Scripture was harmonious with the experience of the early church and that was noted by James.

Further, the decision was compatible with the Great Commission, which commanded that the gospel be taken to "all nations, baptizing them [*not* circumcising them] in the name of the Father and of the Son and of the Holy Spirit" (Matt. 28:19). Decision making in the early church was a group process of theological formation by discussion and debate under competent leadership; it was not a parliamentary power play according to manmade rules. The objective evidence of Scripture and what God was doing experientially in the church were the primary objective criteria for the compromise decision. But equally important was the sensitivity of leaders to people's value systems.

Facts and Feelings

The leaders of the church, namely, Paul, Barnabas, Peter, James, and the other elders and apostles, were sensitive to both objective facts and the strong, subjective value systems and feelings of the believers in the church.

There were objective facts to consider. Gentiles were coming to Christ by the thousands, and Paul and Barnabas testified to these things. Peter had a vision and "God made a choice among you that the Gentiles might hear from my lips the message of the gospel and believe" (Acts 15:7). Undeniably, God "showed that he accepted them by giving the Holy Spirit to them, just as he did to us. He made no distinction between us and them, for he purified their hearts by faith" (Acts 15:8). Some had gone out without authorization and troubled the minds of many by what they had said (Acts 15:24). Scripture verified the intention of God to call Gentiles to himself. All of these things were objective, noted facts.

Yet, there was a keen sensitivity to the value systems and the volatile emotions of the people themselves. There were the strong feelings of Peter: "Now then, why do you try to test God by putting on the necks of the disciples a yoke that neither we nor our fathers have been able to bear? No! We believe it is through the grace of our Lord Jesus that we are saved, just as they are" (Acts 15:10–11). There were also the deep sentiments of Jewish believers who had not yet developed the spiritual perceptivity and maturity of some leaders. They had consciences that needed to be protected. Leaders, particularly James, realized that they could not ignore the deep sensitivities of these brothers. A solution must be found that respected the value systems of all concerned, but that did not ignore objective criteria. It is a testimony to both the providence of God and the spiritual discernment of leaders that such a solution evolved in the discussion process.

Good leaders never ignore facts in favor of sentiment, but neither do they dismiss value systems in favor of objective data. Hard facts and tender feelings are carefully respected. Leaders do not run roughshod over people's feelings in their efforts to get a quick, efficient, calculated decision compatible with objective facts. Neither are decisions made merely on the basis of public sentiment. The best decisions are made under the leadership of those with keen minds capable of evaluating objective facts, those who also have tender hearts, sensitive to subjective, deeply-held value systems. Such is always the genius of spiritual servant-leadership.

Summary

A study of Acts 15 reveals how the church made a difficult policy decision on an extremely volatile issue. An excellent decision evolved out of the process of much discussion, prayer, and biblical research. Most of the normative, philosophic tenets of good church leadership are exhibited in this instructive passage. Leaders were committed to scriptural guidance and group process, including fervent and prolonged debate, compromise, respect for facts and feelings, and consensus.

Today's spiritual leader would be wise to take note of how the early church resolved a thorny, divisive issue with a high degree of satisfaction for the entire church.

Bibliography

Adams, Jay. *Pastoral Leadership*. Grand Rapids: Baker, 1975.

————— . *Shepherding God's Flock*. Grand Rapids: Baker, 1980.

Armerding, Hudson T. *Leadership*. Wheaton: Tyndale House, 1978.

Bannerman, Douglas. *The Scripture Doctrine of the Church*. Grand Rapids: Baker, 1976.

Barber, Cyril J., and Gary H. Strauss. *Leadership: The Dynamics of Success*. Greenwood, S.C.: Attic, 1982.

Bellah, Robert N., et al. *Habits of the Heart: Individualism and Commitment in American Life*. New York: Harper and Row, 1985.

Bloesch, Donald G. *Crumbling Foundations*. Grand Rapids: Zondervan, 1984.

Bonhoeffer, Dietrich. *Life Together*. New York: Macmillan, 1954.

Bruce, F. F. *The Acts of the Apostles*. Philadelphia: Inter-Varsity Christian Fellowship, 1952.

Burns, James. *Leadership*. New York: Harper and Row, 1979.

Bustanoby, Andre. *You Can Change Your Personality: Make It a Spiritual Asset*. Grand Rapids: Zondervan, 1976.

Campolo, Anthony, Jr. *The Power Delusion*. Wheaton: Victor, 1983.

Coates, Thomas. *Authority in the Church*. St. Louis: Concordia, 1964.

Colson, Charles. *The Struggle for Men's Hearts and Minds*. Wheaton: Victor, 1986.

Dale, Robert D. *Ministers as Leaders*. Nashville: Broadman, 1984.

————— . *Pastoral Leadership*. Nashville: Abingdon, 1986.

Ehninger, Douglas, and Wayne Brockridge. *Decision by Debate*. New York: Dodd, Mead, 1963.

Elliott, Grace. *How to Help Groups Make Decisions*. New York: Association, 1959.

Engstrom, Ted W. *The Making of a Christian Leader*. Grand Rapids: Zondervan, 1976.

Engstrom, Ted W., and Edward Dayton. *The Christian Executive*. Waco: Word, 1979.

Fisher, B. Aubrey. *Small Group Decision Making: Communication and Group Process*. New York: McGraw-Hill, 1974.

Frazier, Claude A. *Should Preachers Play God?* Independence, Mo.: Independence Press, 1973.

Freeley, Austin J. *Argumentation and Debate*. Belmont, Calif.: Wadsworth, 1981.

Gabriel, H. W. *Twenty Steps to Power, Influence and Control Over People*. Englewood Cliffs, N.J.: Prentice-Hall, 1962.

Gangel, Kenneth O. *Building Leaders for Church Education*. Chicago: Moody, 1981.

————— . *Competent to Lead*. Chicago: Moody, 1974.

Gardner, John W. *The Heart of the Matter: Leader-Constituent Interaction*. Washington, D.C.: Independent Sector, 1986.

————— . *Leadership and Power*. Washington, D.C.: Independent Sector, 1986.

————— . *The Moral Aspect of Leadership*. Washington, D.C.: Independent Sector, 1987.

————— . *The Nature of Leadership: Introductory Considerations*. Washington, D.C.: Independent Sector, 1986.

————— . *The Tasks of Leadership*. Washington, D.C.: Independent Sector, 1986.

Glasse, James. *Profession: Minister*. Nashville: Abingdon, 1968.

Gordon, Thomas. *Group-Centered Leadership*. Boston: Houghton Mifflin, 1955.

————— . *Leader Effectiveness Training*. New York: Wyden, 1977.

Gouran, Dennis S. *Discussion: The Process of Group Decision-Making*. New York: Harper and Row, 1974.

Greenleaf, Robert. *Servant Leadership*. New York: Paulist, 1977.

Grove, Andrew. *High Output Management*. New York: Random House, 1983.

Guthrie, Donald. *New Testament Theology*. Downers Grove: Inter-Varsity, 1981.

Harris, John. *Stress, Power, and Ministry*. Washington, D.C.: Alban Institute, 1979.

Hasling, John. *Group Discussion and Decision Making.* New York: Thomas Y. Crowell, 1975.

Hersey, Paul, and Kenneth Blanchard. *Management of Organizational Behavior.* Englewood Cliffs, N.J.: Prentice-Hall, 1982.

Hughes, Kent, and Barbara Hughes. *Liberating Ministry from the Success Syndrome.* Wheaton: Tyndale House, 1987.

Jefferson, Charles. *The Ministering Shepherd.* Paris: Young Men's Christian Association, 1912.

Jennings, Eugene. *An Anatomy of Leadership.* New York: McGraw-Hill, 1972.

Johnson, Luke T. *Decision Making in the Church.* Philadelphia: Fortress, 1983.

Jones, Ilion. *The Pastor: The Man and His Ministry.* Philadelphia: Westminister, 1961.

Kittel, Gerhard, ed. *Theological Dictionary of the New Testament.* Grand Rapids: Eerdmans, 1964.

LaPiere, Richard. *Theory of Social Control.* New York: McGraw-Hill, 1954.

Lightfoot, J. B. *The Christian Ministry.* New York: Macmillan, 1901.

Locke, Edwin, and Gary Latham. *Goal Setting.* Englewood Cliffs, N.J.: Prentice-Hall, 1984.

Lundborg, Louis B. *The Art of Being an Executive.* New York: Free Press, 1981.

Maccoby, Michael. *The Leader.* New York: Ballantine, 1981.

McCall, Morgan, Jr., and Michael Lombardo, eds. *Leadership: Where Else Can We Go?* Durham, N.C.: Duke University Press, 1978.

McClelland, David C. *Power: The Inner Experience.* New York: Irvington, 1975.

McConkey, Dale. *How to Manage by Results.* New York: American Management Associations, 1983.

Moberg, David O. *The Church as a Social Institution.* Grand Rapids: Baker, 1984.

Moore, John, and Ken Neff. *A New Testament Blueprint for the Chruch.* Chicago: Moody, 1985.

Niebuhr, H. Richard. *The Purpose of the Church and Its Ministry.* New York: Harper and Brothers, 1956.

Niebuhr, H. Richard, and Daniel D. Williams, eds. *The Ministry in Historical Perspective.* New York: Harper and Brothers, 1956.

Paul, Robert S. *Ministry.* Grand Rapids: Eerdmans, 1965.

Pentecost, Dwight. *The Joy of Living.* Grand Rapids: Zondervan, 1973.

Peters, Thomas, and Robert Waterman. *In Search of Excellence.* New York: Warner, 1982.

Purkiser, W. T. *The New Testament Image of the Ministry.* Grand Rapids: Baker, 1970.

Quayle, William A. *The Pastor-Preacher.* Grand Rapids: Baker, 1979.

Rahner, Karl. *Theology of Pastoral Action.* New York: Herder and Herder. 1968.

Raines, Robert A. *New Life in the Church*. New York: Harper and Row, 1961.

Ramm, Bernard. *The Pattern of Authority*. Grand Rapids: Eerdmans, 1957.

Richards, Larry, and Clyde Hoeldtke. *A Theology of Church Leadership*. Grand Rapids: Zondervan, 1980.

Robinson, Jerry, and Roy Clifford. *Leadership Roles in Community Groups*. Urbana-Champaign, Ill.: University of Illinois, 1975.

Rush, Myron. *Management: A Biblical Approach*. Wheaton: Victor, 1983.

Sanders, J. Oswald. *Spiritual Leadership*. Chicago: Moody, 1967.

Sanford, John. *Ministry Burnout*. New York: Paulist, 1982.

Saucy, Robert. *The Church in God's Program*. Chicago: Moody, 1972.

Schaller, Lyle E. *The Decision-Makers*. Nashville: Abingdon, 1974.

Schuller, David S., Milo L. Brekke, and Merton P. Strommen. *Readiness for Ministry*, vol. 1 and 2. Vandalia, Ohio: The Association of Theological Schools in the United States and Canada, 1975.

Selznick, Philip. *Leadership and Administration*. Berkeley: University of California Press, 1984.

Smith, Donald. *Clergy in the Cross-Fire*. Philadelphia: Westminster, 1978.

Southard, Samuel. *Pastoral Authority in Personal Relationships*. Nashville: Abingdon, 1969.

Spurgeon, Charles. *All-Round Ministry*. Reprint ed. Carlisle, Penn.: Banner of Truth, 1972.

————— . *Lectures to My Students*. Reprint ed. Grand Rapids: Zondervan, 1954.

Steele, David A. *Images of Leadership and Authority for the Church*. New York: University Press of America, 1986.

Stogdill, Ralph. *Handbook of Leadership*. New York: Free Press, 1974.

Stott, John R. W. *The Preacher's Portrait*. Grand Rapids: Eerdmans, 1961.

Swindoll, Charles. *Hand Me Another Brick*. Nashville: Nelson, 1978.

————— . *Leadership*. Waco: Word, 1985.

Tillapaugh, Frank. *The Church Unleashed*. Ventura, Calif.: Regal, 1982.

Trecker, Harleigh, and Audrey Trecker. *Working with Groups, Committees, and Communities*. Chicago: Follett, 1979.

Trueblood, Elton. *The Incendiary Fellowship*. New York: Harper and Row. 1967.

Williams, Daniel. *The Minister and the Care of Souls*. New York: Harper and Row, 1961.

Zaleznik, Abraham. *Human Dilemmas of Leadership*. New York: Harper and Row, 1966.

Index

inadequate relational skills, 12
inspiring spiritual growth, 65–66, 69
laissez-faire leadership, 74–75, 81
laity, role in, 20, 23–28, 30
leaders, defined, 23–30
management of church, 61–62
misuse of prerogatives, 12
participatory leadership, 74, 78, 80, 86
people consciousness, 62–63, 68
performance evaluation, 57–69
policy making, 91–103
priorities in leadership, 67–69
qualifications for leadership, 32–36
rejection of leadership, 37–41
resistance to leadership, 12
role models, 49–50
selection of leaders, 27
servility or hostility, 81–82
stewardship of leaders, 50–51
strategies of leadership, 62–69
style of leadership, 74–78, 82–88
submissive leadership, 75, 77–82
team spirit, 64–65, 69
testing spiritual leadership, 123–36
trustworthiness, 32
undermining confidence, 81
unity and cohesiveness, 12–13, 17, 19
vacuum in leadership, 86–87
vision of role in leadership, 61, 68
weaknesses in, 17, 19–22, 30
See also Crisis in leadership; Decision
    making; Elders and deacons;
    Government of the church; Power
    struggle for authority; Style of
    leadership
Lightfoot, J. B., 24
Lombardo, Michael, 31
Lundborg, Louis B., 60

McCall, Morgan, Jr., 31
Materialism, secularization of church,
    39–40

Newsweek, 39
Niebuhr, H. Richard, 39, 49, 115

Pastors and leadership
    ambiguity, confusion, and conflict,
        45–46
    appropriate leadership power, 109–14
    authority, 114–17

burnout, dropout, 12, 30
clerical leadership, 23–30
communication ability, 12
dropouts, 12, 21, 30
effectiveness of spiritual leadership,
    123–33
guiding to maturity, 113–14
inspiring spiritual growth, 65–66, 69
leadership role, 44, 49–50
manner alienating others, 20–21
pastor, defined, 25
relational skills, 12–13
servant-leadership relationship, 35–36,
    42–48
short pastorates, 12, 20–21
spiritual leadership, 33–35, 37, 46–47,
    49–51
submission to authority, 117–20
training, 13
Paul
    aggressive leadership, 75, 87
    church administration, 130–31
    decision making, 26–28, 132, 142, 158,
        170, 172–73, 177, 181
    effective leadership, 17
    elders, role in church, 26
    evangelism, 27
    Gentiles and Christianity, 187–89, 194,
        196, 198–99
    inspiring spiritual growth, 66
    leadership role, 64
    model of Christian discipleship,
        110–11
    philosophy of ministry, 125–26
    policy-making authority, 96, 102
    spiritual leadership, 34–35, 37, 46–47,
        49–51
    stewardship of leaders, 50
    teaching scriptural truths, 111–12
Peter, decision making, 188, 191, 194,
    196, 198–99
Peters, Thomas, 18, 66
Policy making
    biblical directions for balance, 93–103
    granting of authority, 94–97
    servant-leadership balance, 97–100
Power struggle for authority, 12, 32,
    39–40
    authority of clergy, 114–17
    bribery and politics, 108
    deception and distortion, 106–7